Webster's Medical Dictionary & First Aid Guide

First Aid Guide begins on page 111

abdomen, abdominal cavity That part of the human body comprising the lower portion of the ***trunk***.
For a more detailed description, see the ***FIRST AID GUIDE****, A Short Course in Anatomy.*

abduct To move away from the midline of the body

abduction The movement of a limb or part of a limb away from the midline of the body, as, for example, when the arm is lifted away from the side of the body. Separation of the fingers or toes is also called abduction. See also, ***adduction.***

abductor A muscle that serves to move a limb such as an arm or leg away from the midline of the body or a body part.

aberrant Deviating from the usual or normal, as *aberrant behavior (of a mental patient).*

aberration A deviation from the norm, as an unusual change in mental state or imperfect vision caused by illness or injury.

ablation Separation or removal of diseased or damaged tissue by surgery.

ablution Washing of the body.

abnormal Descriptive of that which is unusual; not conforming to the normal.

abnormality A condition that is not usual or typical, such as a behavioral problem, an irregularity in the function of an organ, or a change in bodily cellular matter.

abortifacient Causing abortion. Something that induces abortion.

abortion A spontaneous abortion, or miscarriage.
A medical termination of pregnancy.
An aborted fetus.

abradant An abrasive.

abrade To wear down by rubbing, as of the skin.

abrasion The process of wearing away by rubbing.

An injury caused by rubbing the surface of the skin.

abscess A swollen, inflamed area of body tissue, often tender or painful, in which pus has gathered.

An abscess is the result of the body's natural response to bacterial infection or an irritant, such as a splinter. ***Leukocytes***, or white blood cells gather in the area to fight the infection. As the dead bacteria, dead leukocytes, etc. build up to form ***pus***, they create pressure and discomfort. Pressing along the line of least resistance, the abscess pushes toward the surface. Eventually, it will burst of its own accord, but may be lanced by a doctor. It is inadvisable to attempt to puncture the abscess before it is ready, as such action may spread the infection.

absorb To take in, as through the pores.

absorbafacient An agent that prompts or increases absorption.

absorbent A substance suited to absorbing.

absorption The process of assimilating food or other substances into the body. Absorption may take place by a number of means, as through the gastro–intestinal tract, through the skin, or through the mucous membranes of the eyes, nose, etc.

Food and drink taken by mouth pass through the esophagus to the stomach, and finally to the small intestine where the bulk of the absorption of food takes place.

Many drugs are absorbed in the same way: taken by mouth, they are carried to the small intestine where they pass through the intestinal wall and enter the bloodstream. Drugs can also be absorbed through the skin and the mucous membranes.

Light rays are likewise absorbed by the body through the skin.

accommodation The adjustment of the lens of the eyes to adapt to available light so as to see clearly in bright or subdued light, and to distinguish objects that are near and those that are far away.

When looking at a close object, the lens of the eye thickens and becomes more convex in order to focus the light from that object on the ***retina***; for a distant object, the lens contracts to bring light from the object into focus.

Over the years, the lens may lose some of its elasticity, limiting the ability to focus, often evidenced by the tendency to hold reading matter further away or the need to wear glasses for reading.

accretion The growing together of usually separated parts.

Achilles tendon The tendon that attaches the heel to the muscles of the calf of the leg.

acne An inflammation of the sebaceous glands, the oil–secreting organs of the skin, manifested by eruptions of hard, inflamed pimples. The condition is most common among teenagers. The oil, sebum, is a fatty substance that normally helps maintain the texture of the skin.

Increased production of androgens, or male sex hormones, in both males and females during puberty causes the sebaceous glands to become especially active and secrete large amounts of sebum that is unusually thick. This sebum has a tendency to block the glands and hair follicles, clogging them with sebum and cellular debris.

Usually the condition is only alleviated by time, fading as the individual reaches adulthood.

Washing gently with a mild soap and water often helps by removing some of the bacteria and debris. Medication is sometimes effective for reducing symptoms, as is exposure to sunlight that tends to dry up the eruptions.

acoustic nerve The nerve that serves the ear.

acquired That which is developed or modified by environmental influence, in contrast to inherited.

acquired immune deficiency syndrome See ***AIDS***

acrophobia An excessive dread of high places. Some fear of heights is natural in reflection of the possible consequences of falling. Acrophobia, however, is an unreasonable fear, as the acrophobic may be terrified even where the possibility of falling is nil.

ACTH AdrenoCorticoTropic Hormone, an essential hormone produced by the pituitary gland located at the base of the brain.

ACTH provides the link between the pituitary gland and the cortex, or covering, of the adrenal glands that secretes vital hormones essential for maintaining the body's biochemical balance. See also, ***endocrinology.***

acupuncture The ancient technique of inserting the tips of long needles into the skin and manipulating them to relieve pain or treat disease.

acute Sudden or severe, although of short duration, as contrasted to ***chronic***.

Addison's disease A condition that occurs when the adrenal glands cease to function properly and fail to produce adequate quantities of the hormones called steroids. Symptoms of Addison's disease are weakness, fatigue, and increased skin pigmentation and may include weight loss, dehydration, low blood pressure, and nausea.

adduction The movement of a limb or part of a limb toward the midline of the body, as, for example, when an outstretched arm is brought back to the side of the body. Similarly, bringing a separated finger or toe back to its normal position is called adduction.

The muscles involved in such movement are referred to as *adductors*. See also, ***abduction.***

adenitis Inflammation of a lymph gland or node.

Lymph glands are scattered throughout the body, mainly concentrated at the side of the neck, in the armpits and in the groin, to aid the body in defending against infection.

adenocarcinoma A common form of cancerous tumor, originating in glandular tissue, mainly in the stomach, large intestine, gallbladder, pancreas, uterus or prostate gland. They may also start in the breast or lungs.

If not detected and treated promptly, adenocarcinomas commonly spread to other parts of the body via the blood or lymphatic systems. The secondary tumor formed by such spreading has the same appearance as that of the original tumor, often aiding in further diagnosis if the location of the original tumor is unknown.

adenoids A mass of lymphoid tissue located at the entrance to the throat above the tonsils. The adenoids contain specialized white blood cells that help provide protection against diseases of the respiratory system.

Adenoids may become enlarged by throat infections as the tonsils do, and sometimes, after repeated infections or allergies, they remain enlarged obstructing the nasal passage. There is reluctance to remove them by surgery, however, because of the protective nature of their function and the fact that they begin to shrink at an early age, so that they are usually gone during adolescence.

adenoma A benign, or non–malignant tumor originating in glandular tissue, as contrasted to ***adenocarcinoma.***

An adenoma is usually harmless as it will not spread or destroy other tissue, although it may cause discomfort.

adenosis Disease of a gland, particularly the abnormal development of glandular tissue.

adipose tissue Fatty tissue that occurs throughout the body, mainly directly under the skin, acting as an insulation and a source of energy. It is thickest in those parts of the body most liable to sudden trauma, such as the buttocks and feet where it acts as a shock absorber.

Adipose tissue in bone marrow supports the arteries and

veins, in the joints and muscles it deters injury from sudden shock, it provides cushion and support for the heart and lungs, it keeps the intestines warm, and it protects the kidneys from shock. An excess, however, can be dangerous, particularly around the heart or lungs where it adds weight to the organ and restricts its movement.

adjuvant A substance added to a medication to intensify its action.

adrenal gland One of the two glands that each lie above a kidney and secrete hormones to control certain functions of the body.

Hormones from the adrenal glands assist in the maintenance of the body's fluid balance, enhance the body's ability to cope with stress, and are vital to regulation of metabolism and sexual development.

aerobe A microorganism that requires oxygen.

aftercare Care or treatment of one who is convalescing.

agoraphobia An irrational fear of open or public places.

Fear of leaving a place considered safe, as the home, manifested by a feeling of panic, often accompanied by a rapid heartbeat, sweating and trembling.

AIDS Acquired Immune Deficiency Syndrome, a disease that attacks the body's immune system rendering it unable to fight disease.

AIDS is caused by a microorganism called the human immunodeficiency virus (HIV), transmitted in body fluids through sexual intercourse, non–sterile hypodermic needles, and contact with infected blood. A pregnant woman may also transmit the disease to a fetus.

Early symptoms include low grade fever, swollen lymph nodes, fatigue, weight loss, and diarrhea. The AIDS victim is susceptible to many diseases, including various cancers, skin infections, and fungal infections. Many of the victims of AIDS develop a cancer known as Kaposi's sarcoma, which appears as purplish bumps on the skin.

Some victims may be carriers without exhibiting any symptoms of the disease. Blood tests can indicate exposure to the disease, although not all individuals with positive test results will contract AIDS.

It is possible to limit the potential for exposure to the virus by restricting the number of one's sexual partners, using condoms, and avoiding contact with hypodermic needles or blood that may be contaminated.

There is no evidence to indicate that the virus is transmitted through casual contact with an infected person.

albinism A condition characterized by a lack of natural pigment in the skin, causing an unnaturally pale appearance. The victim has low tolerance for exposure to sun and may exhibit an excessive sensitivity to bright light.

albumin One of the two major proteins of the blood, formed in the liver from ingested food. Albumin is water–soluble and found in a variety of forms in animals, egg white and vegetables. See also, ***globulin.***

albuminuria The presence of ***albumin*** in the urine, often a sign of kidney malfunction. ***Proteinuria*** is virtually the same as albuminuria, since albumin is the only protein detected in significant amounts in the urine.

alcohol A colorless, volatile liquid. *Alcohol* refers to any of a class of organic compounds containing one or more hydroxyl groups, as *ethyl alcohol*, obtained by the fermentation of sugar, used in medicine and beverages, or *methyl alcohol*, synthesized from carbon monoxide and hydrogen, used as a fuel or solvent.

alcoholism A disease caused by the excess consumption of alcoholic beverages.

Small doses of alcohol cause a feeling of relaxation, some loss of inhibitions and stimulation of the appetite. Larger doses can impair speech and coordination, and may irritate the stomach lining. A very large amount can produce severe depression of the central nervous system and may be fatal. Regular ingestion of large quantities of alcohol can create a dependency and have injurious effects on the organs of the body, especially of the liver.

alkalosis An excessive concentration of alkali, or bicarbonate, in the body fluids. *Metabolic alkalosis* normally is the result of the loss of hydrochloric acid from the stomach caused by protracted vomiting or taking an excessive amount of antacids for an upset stomach. Usually, the condition is alleviated when the kidneys have enough fluid to adjust the amount of alkali in the blood. *Respiratory alkalosis* is caused by excessive exhalation of carbon dioxide, usually caused by rapid hysterical breathing that can often be corrected by breathing into a paper bag so that carbon dioxide breathed out is breathed in again. Alkalosis may be characterized by dizziness and jerky muscular contractions.

allergen Any substance that causes an allergic response in the body's immune system.

allergy Excessive sensitivity to a substance, as pollen, feathers, or dust, or a chemical.

Allergy is the cause of hay fever and hives, and may be the cause of many cases of asthma, eczema and sinusitis.

Allergic reactions are an exaggeration of the customary immune response to bacteria, virus, etc.

Allergic reactions are most common in the respiratory tract and the skin, although they may also affect the digestive system.

allergy and immunology The study of the diagnosis and treatment of disorders that relate to the body's ability to resist threatening substances.

Immunologists, for example, may search for ways modify the immune system to reject cancerous growth or to accept an organ transplant.

Those who deal with allergies are concerned with identifying irritants that cause symptoms and devising treatment. Allergies may be alleviated by a change of environment, the use of drugs to relieve symptoms, or a program of desensitization.

Alzheimer's disease A disease caused by presenile brain atrophy, the premature shrinking of the brain that causes slowing of the mental processes, beginning with forgetfulness and progressing to irrationality.

Early symptoms are small memory lapses, usually involving lack of recall for recent events. As the disease progresses, a person may forget names of close relatives or friends, get lost in familiar places, regularly misplace articles, recheck tasks that have been done, or repeatedly ask questions that have already been answered.

As the disease worsens, the victim becomes confused, frustrated, and irritable. Endless repetition of actions is also characteristic. Some victims become extremely agitated with little or no apparent provocation.

amblyopia Defective eyesight without any apparent defect of the eye. The condition may be temporary or permanent, and it may be partial or result in total blindness.

Amblyopia may be caused by poisons, as from alcohol, tobacco, lead, petroleum derivatives, etc. Strokes often cause some loss of vision when there is damage to the portion of the brain that controls eyesight.

amenorrhea Absence of menstruation. *Primary amenorrhea* refers to a condition in which menstruation has never occurred. *Secondary amenorrhea* refers to a cessation of menstruation in a woman who has previously been menstruating, commonly caused by pregnancy and lactation. It may also be due to anemia brought on by heavy menstrual blood loss in the past, ovarian failure, certain pituitary diseases, an emotional disturbance, or even a disruptive change in life style.

amentia Mental retardation; a congenital mental deficiency. See also, ***dementia***.

amino acid Any of the group of organic compounds that form the basic constituents of protein.

amnesia A loss of memory, temporary or permanent, caused by damage to the brain or psychological reaction. An injury to the head that involves loss of consciousness may result in some loss of memory of a period before and after the injury. Memory may return as the victim recovers, but parts of memory may never be recovered. Similar loss of memory can occur in the case of severe ***trauma***, or injury, that does not involve the head.

Abrupt memory loss without injury or illness is usually the result of a psychological disorder; a person wandering aimlessly with no recollection is probably suffering from *hysterical amnesia* brought on by emotional stress.

Memory for most of one's life is, for the most part, continuous. In old age, memory of recent events may be faulty, while memories from the past remain intact.

Short–term memory loss is also a symptom of chronic alcoholism and some brain diseases such as Alzheimer's.

amniocentesis Drawing off a sample of the amniotic fluid from the womb of a pregnant woman in order to examine it. Amniotic fluid is the medium in which the fetus lies and contains some cells from the fetus that can be analyzed to detect a number of abnormalities.

amputation The cutting off of a part of the body, usually a limb or part of a limb.

anabolism Conversion of food into living tissue by the body; part of the metabolic process. See also, ***catabolism***.

analgesia Relief from pain without loss of consciousness. *Analgesics,* or drugs that produce analgesia, are of three types: those that act directly on the source of the pain, those that act on the brain, and those that are specific, that act in the presence of a particular illness or disease.

The most common analgesics are the first group, such as acetaminophen or aspirin, used to combat relatively mild pain. Aspirin is also known for its ability to reduce fever and inflammation. Acetaminophen is milder, but not as effective for reducing fever or inflammation.

The second group, far more potent, with a potential for abuse, are dispensed by prescription. They include substances such as morphine, methadone, and codeine.

The analgesics in the third group act on specifics, such as migraine or certain types of neuralgia.

Analgesia can also be uncontrolled, as from a disease of the sensory system or from an overdose of alcohol.

anaphylactic shock A severe reaction of the body to certain vaccines, antibiotics, insect stings, or other antigens that may cause a state of total collapse.

For more detailed information, see the ***FIRST AID GUIDE***, *Shock*.

androgen A substance that promotes the development of secondary male characteristics.

anemia A shortage of red blood cells or a deficiency of hemoglobin, the pigment in red blood cells that carries oxygen throughout the body.

Symptoms are not distinctive, and the condition may not be detected unless it is severe. The sufferer may experience fatigue, shortness of breath, loss of appetite, dizziness, and weakness. Very severe cases may exhibit swollen ankles, a rapid weak pulse, and pale clammy skin.

Anemia can be caused by inadequate materials for the manufacture of red blood cells, such as by poor diet, loss of iron in excessive bleeding, or disease that renders the body unable to absorb the vital materials; the inability of bone marrow to manufacture the cells, caused by disease, exposure to radioactivity, or drugs; excessive or untimely destruction of the cells, by excessive bleeding, disease, infection, or a mismatched blood transfusion; or inherited abnormalities such as *sickle cell anemia*.

Conditions such as bleeding ulcers, cancer, and alcoholism are likely to cause one or more types of anemia.

anesthesia A diminished or lost sense of feeling, especially of the sensations of pain and touch.

Anesthesia can be brought on by disease, trauma, damage to the nervous system, or the action of drugs.

Anesthesia usually refers to the administering of a drug to produce a reduced state of sensitivity in order to perform a surgical operation, or to the drug so administered.

anesthesiology The science of the administration of drugs to reduce or limit sensitivity.

aneurysm A bulge or swelling in an artery weakened by disease or injury. The primary danger associated with an aneurysm is that of rupture of the blood vessel, causing internal bleeding that can prove fatal.

Aneurysms occur most often in the aorta, the largest artery in the body, the artery behind the knee, and the arteries at the base of the brain. The aneurysm may be detected in the abdomen as a pulsating mass that is very tender, and at the back of the knee as one that is painful. In a neck artery, there may be interference with nerves serving the eye, causing double vision as well as a pulsating sound that the sufferer may detect.

A *dissecting aneurysm* is one in which the blood runs between the walls of the artery, sometimes eventually reentering the main vessel. A dissecting aneurysm in the chest will cause severe pain in the area and often symptoms resembling a heart attack.

In the abdomen, pain may be severe in the area of an

aneurysm and radiate to the back, accompanied by a loss of blood flow to the legs.

angina pectoris A dull pressure or pain in the center of the chest that may be accompanied by a burning sensation not unlike indigestion, and a radiating tingle down the left arm indicating that the heart muscle is not getting enough oxygen, as during a period of stress or exertion.

The pain is usually not as severe as that of a heart attack, and the heart muscles are not damaged. The pain will usually recede quickly if the victim stops all activity.

An attack of angina is not a heart attack, but the experience indicates that the individual is a likely candidate.

The most common condition that deprives the heart muscle of adequate blood and oxygen is a narrowing of the coronary artery due to ***atherosclerosis***. Physical or mental stress can hasten the onset. Whatever the suspected cause, a physician should be consulted.

Angina is usually treated by altering lifestyle to reduce stress and strain on the heart. Smoking, overeating and overexertion should be avoided. Regular exercise is necessary, but should be tailored to the condition, avoiding activities that place sudden, severe demand on the heart.

angiography An X ray examination of blood vessels that have been injected with a substance opaque to X rays in order to make them visible on the X–ray plate or viewing screen. This technique is also used in the diagnosis of tumors, especially of the brain.

angioma A tumor of mostly blood and lymph vessels.

angioplasty Any of a number of surgical techniques for repairing damaged blood vessels.

ankylosis A condition characterized by stiffness or immobility of a joint caused by fusion of its parts as a consequence of injury or surgery.

anorexia A lack of appetite, or desire for food.

anorexia nervosa An *aversion* to food that usually begins in an attempt to lose weight, but is carried to extremes. The individual may suffer from severe vitamin and mineral deficiency, often worsened by induced vomiting, the use of purgatives, and excessive exercise. If allowed to continue, the victim will literally starve to death while convinced that his or her diet is adequate.

anthrax An infectious disease that commonly infects cattle, goats or sheep and can be transmitted to man.

Humans contract the infection from spores that survive in contaminated wool, hair or hides. Hygienic methods of handling these materials have diminished the disease.

Infection can affect the skin, where it is characterized by itching pustules that turn black as the infection spreads. The infection also has a tendency to attack the lungs.

antibody A chemical compound produced by the body to neutralize a particular foreign substance, called an ***antigen***, entering the body. The antibody created is unique, effective only in defense against that antigen. Its purpose is to overcome an attack and to ward off future attacks.

The first time a particular bacteria invades, the body formulates an antibody. By the time the infection has run its course, there are often enough of the antibodies remaining in the blood to ward off a further attack, perhaps for life. Such is the basis for immunization, that introduces dead or weakened bacteria into the body so that it will develop the necessary antibodies while experiencing few or none of the symptoms of the disease.

antigen Any substance the immune system identifies as a threat that starts the reaction leading to production of a special ***antibody***. Antigens are contained in bacteria and viruses, blood from an incompatible blood group, and sera injected into the body for the treatment or prevention of infectious disease.

antipyretic A medication that tends to reduce fever.
antiseptic A substance that inhibits the action of bacteria.
antitoxin A substance that neutralizes a specific toxin that is released by bacteria.
anuria Lack of urination caused by kidney failure or by a blockage.
anxiety Fear or apprehension about some future possibility. Anxiety is a normal response to anything of concern, the outcome of which is uncertain. It may, however, become excessive and irrational. Concern about making a good impression on others, for example, is a form of normal anxiety. Such anxiety is unhealthy, however, when apprehension is so great that one refuses to meet new people. Excessive anxiety about such things as crime or pollution can trap one in the home without hope of reprieve except with professional help.
aorta The main artery of the body that extends from the left ventricle of the heart.
aphagia A lack of ability to swallow.
aphasia Loss of the ability to speak coherently, especially to connect words and ideas, as from a stroke.
apnea A temporary stopping of breathing.
apoplexy See ***stroke***
appendicitis Inflammation of the appendix, a small growth at the end of the large intestine that serves no apparent purpose.

Appendicitis usually produces a dull or sharp pain in the abdomen that may be intensified by coughing, sneezing, or even moving accompanied by a feeling of nausea and constipation, although diarrhea is not infrequent. As the pain becomes constant, it may move to the lower right side of the abdomen or even to the back. The area around the appendix may become tender. At this stage the appendix is likely to become so swollen that it may burst, infecting surrounding tissue to create a potentially life threatening situation. Symptoms vary, as does the location of the appendix. When there is severe abdominal pain that persists, consult a physician as soon as possible.

arteriosclerosis A condition in which the walls of the arteries are thickened and rigid, rendering them unable to process an adequate supply of blood. Commonly called *hardening of the arteries*. See also, ***atherosclerosis.***

arthritis An inflammation of the ***joints*** that causes swelling, pain, and stiffness. Damp weather, emotional stress, excess weight, and abuse of the joints at work or play can make symptoms more pronounced.

Arthritis is brought about by damage to the smooth surfaces where two bones join. Damage may be caused by injury, a progressive wearing away with age, or illness that pushes the joint out of position.

Most common is *rheumatoid arthritis* which causes inflammation in the synovium, a thin membrane that lines and lubricates the joint. The inflammation ultimately destroys the tissue that lines the joint, replacing it with scar tissue, and the joint becomes swollen and painful.

The most effective treatment for arthritis includes drug therapy, exercise, and rest. Aspirin is the drug most commonly prescribed—two or three tablets several times a day to reduce inflammation and relieve pain. Non-aspirin pain relievers may also be effective. Exercise is important to preserve mobility. Moist heat is often recommended to reduce pain and improve mobility.

arthroplasty The surgical repair or replacement of a joint. In some cases where joints have become stiff and painful as the result of disease or injury, the joint may be excised by cutting away the damaged portions of bone. Such surgery leaves scar tissue to fill the gap and although the pain is relieved, the joint may be unstable.

In other cases, it is possible to replace the joint or a portion of the joint. Replacement surgery has been particularly successful in the replacement of the hip joint.

asbestosis An inflammation of the lungs caused by the inhalation of asbestos particles. Certain types of *asbestos* do not burn or conduct heat or electricity, and are used in heat and fire resistant products, as well as insulation. Asbestosis is commonly contracted by those who work with asbestos or are exposed to fine particles in the air. The particles irritate the lungs and cause shortness of breath and coughing. The victim may also suffer loss of appetite, weight loss, and bouts of fatigue. After a time, the sufferer is likely to contract tuberculosis and cancer.

ascorbic acid See ***Vitamin C***

asepsis The condition of being completely free of germs.

asphyxia Suffocation.

A lack of oxygen in the blood caused by interference with respiration usually involving loss of consciousness.

Drowning is probably the most common incidence when water blocks the passage of air to the lungs. The passage may also be shut off by accidental inhalation of food, blockage by swelling from an infection, or strangulation.

Other causes include inhalation of air containing too little oxygen or poison gases, and electric shock.

asthenia A loss or lack of body strength or stamina.

asthma A respiratory disorder characterized by difficulty in breathing. Asthma attacks may be set off by allergy, infection, overexertion, inhaling cold air, or stress.

Normally, air enters the lungs and is expelled through the tiny bronchioles at the end of the bronchi. The asthmatic's difficulty is caused by sensitivity of the bronchioles that brings about constriction or clogging so that spent air cannot be properly expelled.

Attacks are unpredictable: they may last a few minutes to

a week or more, they may occur regularly or only occasionally, and they may be mild or extremely severe.

astigmatism A condition of the eye in which imperfect curvature of the cornea or lens prevents the image on the retina from focusing clearly and parts of the image appear blurred. Although the blurring may not be apparent, the eye must constantly readjust to correct the image, causing it to tire quickly, one of the primary symptoms.

ataxia Lack of muscle coordination.

Ataxia may be congenital, that is, existing from birth, or caused by injury or disease of the central nervous system. Ataxia is characterized by irregular movements of the body that are unsteady or clumsy, as of an awkward manner of walking with feet wide apart, or a seeming lack of balance

atherosclerosis A condition in which arterial blood flow is blocked by fatty deposits; the most common form of ***arteriosclerosis***, or hardening of the arteries, and a major contributor to heart attacks and strokes.

Formation begins when the concentration of fats necessary for proper function of the body and always present in the bloodstream is greatly increased and forms fatty streaks on the artery wall. The streaks attract nodules of cholesterol. Scar tissue forms under the nodules and in turn attracts calcium deposits that create a hard material called plaque. The lining of plaque restricts ability of the artery to expand and contract properly and interferes with the flow of blood. Clots may form, further restricting blood flow, and in extreme cases, cutting it off entirely.

Atherosclerosis is not usually apparent until the arteries leading to a vital organ are partially blocked or closed off completely. Symptoms then relate to the organ that has been cut off—stoppage of blood to the heart, for example, will trigger a heart attack; closing off arteries to the head may cause dizziness, blindness, or a stroke.

Aside for treatment of symptoms caused by atherosclerosis, and surgical procedure to bypass clogged arteries, the only remedy for the disease is prevention, such as losing weight, reducing harmful fat in the diet, avoiding smoking, and exercising in moderation.

athlete's foot A fungal infection of the foot characterized by an itching, burning, or stinging feeling, especially between the toes where the skin often reddens and cracks. Peeling of the skin may occur as well.

Treatment generally involves application of salves, powders, or liquids available from the drugstore.

Athlete's foot can usually be prevented by eliminating the warm, moist environment in which the fungus thrives. The key is to dry feet well, especially between the toes, after taking a shower; change socks often and rotate shoes, especially in the hot, humid summer months; and use powder to keep the feet dry.

Athlete's foot is contagious. If it's necessary to use public showers, as in a health club, clogs should be worn and the feet dusted with an anti–fungal powder afterwards.

In spite of caution, athlete's foot may easily be contracted and will often recur. If recurrence is frequent and severe, a physician should be consulted to verify that the problem is not caused by infection with similar symptoms, such as an allergic reaction to chemicals in the shoes.

atrophy The degeneration or wasting away of an organ or part of the body, as from disease or disuse.

auscultation Listening, as with a stethoscope to sounds within the body; or the study of such sounds.

Sounds are made within the body, especially by the heart and lungs, that are characteristic of normal operation. By auscultation, a physician with the aid of a stethoscope for amplification is able to distinguish those sounds from others that may be indicators of malfunction.

autism A condition characterized by a preoccupation with fantasy and lack of concern for reality.

An early sign of autism is indifference to those who give care, as lack of response to affection. There may be little or no interest in learning to eat, use the toilet, or speak, though there is no difficulty in learning to walk.

Such children may have an excellent memory and a high level of intelligence, but no apparent concern or desire to interact with those around them. Change, such as rearranging furniture, is upsetting to them. It appears that perception of the everyday world is distorted and frightening, so that they seek that which is familiar.

autoimmune disease Any of a number of diseases that cause the body's immune system to produce antibodies that attack healthy tissue in the body.

autopsy Examination of a body after death.

The autopsy, also known as a *postmortem examination* or *necropsy*, is conducted by a *pathologist* who dissects the body, usually to determine the cause of death. Permission for the examination may be granted by a close relative, although such examination may be required in the case of death by violence or that of a suspicious nature, depending on state law.

The examination is very methodical, from a thorough survey of the outer surfaces to careful examination of each organ, and includes taking samples of tissue and of the contents of the body, as urine, blood, undigested food, etc. that are kept for laboratory analysis.

backbone See ***spinal column***

bacteria Any of a class of one–celled microscopic organisms, smaller than yeasts and larger than viruses, with a primitive nucleus, that multiplies by splitting in two and is able to multiply outside a living cell.

Some bacteria are especially useful, as those that live in the intestines and aid in digestion, those that enrich the soil, or those used for making wine, beer, cheese, etc. Bacteria that cause disease by invading tissue and then reproducing to destroy their surroundings, or by releasing toxins that poison the body are called *pathogenic*. Bacteria are usually transmitted by direct contact, by contact with contaminated matter, or by insects. Normally, the body is able to protect itself from harmful bacteria, but occasionally requires the assistance of antibiotics that destroy the organisms or prevent their multiplication.

bariatrics The study and treatment of obesity.
In addition to establishing dietary guidelines, the *bariatrician* is concerned with analyzing data related to the condition of being overweight or underweight in order to separate hard scientific evidence from myth.

battered-child syndrome Physical abuse of a child by a parent, guardian, baby sitter, or someone else in a position of trust. Abuse is often deliberate and repeated, and may be provoked by a seemingly inconsequential act. In additional to physical injuries, the child may be deprived of food or comfort, and suffer psychological damage as a result of the abuse.

bedsores Ulcerated sores on the body of person who is bedridden for an extended period; also called *pressure sores* or *decubitus ulcers*.
When the small blood vessels that nourish the skin and underlying tissue are compressed for an extended period, they cease to function and tissue dies. Continued pressure can cause a spread of the condition to a large area and the formation of an ulcer that may become infected. Treatment of bedsores, like prevention, requires relief of the pressure; the patient must be permitted to recuperate on an air bed or in a net hammock.

Bell's palsy A partial or total paralysis of one side of the face. Bell's palsy is characterized by a lop–sided appearance to the face, mainly due to drooping of the mouth on the affected side. Believed to be caused by inflammation of the nerve controlling the facial muscles, the onset of the disease is rapid. Recovery usually occurs in about a week, although it is not always complete.

bends A painful condition in which nitrogen bubbles in the blood block the flow of blood to tissues; a symptom of decompression sickness or caisson disease.

Bends may be experienced by moving too quickly from an area of high pressure to one of lower pressure, as by deep sea divers. It is normal for nitrogen from the atmosphere to dissolve in the blood, but the amount increases as pressure increases. When pressure decreases, nitrogen moves from the blood to the lungs, but the process takes longer, so that if a diver surfaces too rapidly, nitrogen bubbles remain in the blood where they form air locks.

benign Descriptive of a tumor that is not malignant, or that is expected to cause little or no harm to the body.

beriberi A vitamin deficiency disease caused by a lack of thiamine. Beriberi affects the circulation and the nervous system, and in severe cases may cause heart failure.

bile A yellow fluid produced by the liver to aid in digestion, especially of fats.

Bile is produced continuously and stored in the gallbladder until food is ingested, at which time the bile is emptied into the intestine to break down fat into tiny globules that can be passed through the walls of the small intestine into the bloodstream to provide fuel for the body.

If the flow of bile is interrupted because the liver is not functioning properly or because of stoppage, digestion is impaired. Such condition can cause jaundice, a yellowing of the skin and eyes. Although jaundice is not a disease in itself, it is symptomatic of a potentially severe problem and should be referred to a physician.

biopsy Removal of a small specimen of tissue for examination and diagnosis.

biotin See ***Vitamin B complex***

birth defect An abnormality that is present at birth. A birth defect may be *genetic*, that is, inherited from one or both parents, or acquired during pregnancy or at birth.

bleeder Descriptive of a person who bleeds excessively, even from an otherwise insignificant wound.

For more detailed information, see the ***FIRST AID GUIDE***, *Controlling Bleeding.*

blister A collection of fluid, such as serum or blood, under the outer layer of skin. A blister may be caused by friction, as from the foot rubbing against the lining of a shoe; by heat, as from a burn; or by a caustic chemical.

An unbroken blister is little more than a petty annoyance if properly tended once the source of irritation is removed; however, a broken blister must be kept clean to prevent infection. Severe blistering should be referred to a physician for medication.

blood A fluid that runs throughout the body by way of the arteries, veins and capillaries.

For a more detailed description, see the ***FIRST AID GUIDE***, *A Short Course in Anatomy.*

blood clot Gelatinous material formed to stem the flow of blood when a blood vessel is injured.

Normally, blood flows without change in its chemistry; however, when a blood vessel is ruptured and the blood comes into contact with foreign tissue, clotting begins. *Platelets* in the blood, triggered by the contact, release a chemical that begins a chain reaction involving a number of protein constituents in the blood, ending with the conversion of *fibrinogen*, a soluble material, to *fibrin*, that is insoluble. The fibrin is laid down in fine strands that collect white and red cells to form a clot.

blood vessels Any of the passageways that carry blood: the arteries, veins and capillaries.

For a more detailed description, see the ***FIRST AID GUIDE***, *A Short Course in Anatomy*.

boil A painful inflammation of the skin caused by bacterial infection; a *furuncle*.

When ***bacteria*** enter the skin through a hair follicle and multiply while producing toxins, they in turn are attacked by white blood cells, or ***leukocytes*** whose job it is to protect the body from such invasion. As the white blood cells consume the bacteria, a pustule that comprises the center of a boil may form. The pustule is made up of white blood cells and cells destroyed by the bacteria. When the pustule pushes to the surface of the skin and erupts, the boil will drain and heal.

Boils are most often formed on the neck, face, or back, but they can be located anywhere on the skin. As they grow, they become red and hot; pressure exerted on surrounding nerves can cause considerable discomfort.

Normally, a boil will mature on its own; however, frequent applications of a warm moist towel may hasten the process. Care should be taken to keep the area clean, especially after the boil erupts, in order to prevent spread of infection. No attempt should be made to burst a boil prematurely by squeezing, as it may erupt under the skin and create new infection. A particularly severe boil or the presence of numerous boils may be symptomatic of other problems and should be referred to a physician.

When a group of boils connects below the surface of the skin, the formation is called a ***carbuncle***.

botulism A type of food poisoning caused by a bacterium found in improperly canned or preserved food.

In addition to the classic symptoms of food poisoning—nausea, vomiting, and abdominal cramps—toxin produced by the bacteria interferes with the transmission of nerve impulses and can cause irregularities in vision, followed by paralysis of the arms and difficulty breathing.
Botulism can be fatal, so an early diagnosis and referral to a physician is critical.

breastbone A bone at the front of the chest that travels downward from the collarbone and to which the ribs are attached; the *sternum*.

bronchitis Inflammation of the bronchi, or air passages of the lung. When the bronchial tubes that are the air passages between the windpipe and the lungs become infected and swollen, glands in the mucous membrane that lines the tubes increase the secretion of mucus. The cough characteristic of bronchitis is an attempt to expel the excess fluid. In extreme cases, the infection may extend to the lungs and develop into *bronchopneumonia*.
Short term bronchitis, often following an attack of the common cold or influenza is called *acute bronchitis*. In addition to the cough, one who contracts acute bronchitis may experience flu–like symptoms: slight fever, a feeling of general malaise, aching muscles, etc. Treatment usually involves rest, steam inhalations and, if necessary, antibiotics to prevent further infection.
Bronchitis caused by repeated irritation from recurring infection, smoke, dust or other effluence, is termed *chronic bronchitis*. Either condition is overcome only when the source of irritation has been removed. Cigarette smoking is a primary cause of chronic bronchitis. Tobacco smoke interferes with the action of the hairlike fibers that push mucus from the lungs, allowing the mucus and irritants trapped by the mucus to remain in the lungs. Chronic bronchitis often leads to permanent damage to lungs and

heart, and should be referred to the care of a physician.

brucellosis Infection caused by the bacterium *Brucella* contracted from cattle, hogs or goats. Also known as *undulant fever* or *Malta fever*, brucellosis is primarily contracted by persons in contact with animals or involved in meat processing, but it can also be transmitted in unpasteurized milk. Symptoms are similar to those for influenza: fever, headache, chills, and listlessness. The name *undulant fever* comes from a tendency of the condition to undulate, or move in waves, that is, bouts of the fever alternate with periods without symptoms.

bubonic plague A highly contagious epidemic disease transmitted by the bite of infected rat fleas. *Bubonic* derives from a symptom of the disease: a bubo, or swelling, of lymph glands, especially in the armpit or groin. Similarly, characteristic bleeding into the skin that causes dark blotches gave rise to the name *Black Death*. The disease is now generally limited to unsanitary tropical areas, but there are occasional outbreaks in western parts of the United States that are controlled by modern drugs.

bursitis Inflammation of a *bursa*, a small sac that cushions the juncture between moving parts of the body, such as bones, tendons, etc. The bursa contains a lubricating fluid that serves to eliminate friction and promote smooth movement of the joints. The swelling and tenderness from inflammation can cause such severe discomfort that movement is virtually impossible.

Bursitis can be *chronic*, caused by repeated or constant stress on a joint, most commonly the elbow, shoulder or knee; or *acute*, caused by sudden trauma. Immobilizing the joint may allow healing to take place, especially in the case of acute bursitis. Chronic bursitis is usually characterized by permanent damage frequently accompanied by calcium deposits that may render the joint immobile. Moist heat or cold compresses may ease the pain and aspirin or other pain relievers can also be effective. Surgery may be recommended in extreme cases.

bypass To skirt or circumvent, as a graft that passes around a clogged section of artery.

An artery narrowed by ***atherosclerosis*** places an added burden on the organ or tissue it serves that can lead to further damage. In addition, there is the possibility that a blood clot will close the vessel completely, with catastrophic results. In many cases the problem can be resolved by grafting a section taken from another part of the body or by implanting a man–made device to circumvent the damaged section of the natural vessel.

cachexia A weakened, emaciated state of the body caused by prolonged illness.

calcification The abnormal accumulation of calcium salts in body tissue.

calculus A solidified mass, as a stone, that may be formed in the kidneys, gallbladder, or other organ of the body.

callus A thickened growth of the skin; a *callosity*.

A callus is generally seen as protection to an area of the skin subjected to abnormal friction or pressure, as on parts of the hands or on the bottoms of the feet. A callus may become so thick that the skin is inflexible and cracks, causing discomfort. In such a case, remove the source of friction and consult a physician if discomfort is extreme. There are non–prescription medications that will soften the callosity, but removal at home is not advisable because of the danger of infection.

cancer Any type of malignant growth.

Normal cells reproduce methodically in accordance with genetic coding; cancerous growth is uncontrolled, spreading throughout the body, destroying or replacing normal cells. Cancer cells have the unique ability to propagate outside the organ where they originate; the cells may be carried in blood or lymphatic channels to other parts of the body where they attack healthy tissue. While there is no single preventative for cancer, the risk of exposure may be lessened by avoiding known *carcinogens,* or cancer causing agents. Most cancer is treatable, so that early warning is also one of the best lines of defense. Symptoms to look for are: radical changes in bowel or bladder function; a wound that does not heal; unusual bleeding or discharge; chronic indigestion; a thickening lump anywhere on the body; any significant change in body function or formation.

canker sore An ulcerated sore, usually of the lips or lining of the mouth. Canker sores are not contagious, and may be induced by fever, allergy, or injury to the mouth, as from ill–fitting dentures.

cardiology The study of the heart and circulatory system, especially for the diagnosis and treatment of disorders.

capillaries Extremely tiny blood vessels that connect the arteries and the veins.

carbohydrate Any of a number of natural compounds that produce heat and energy, comprising the bulk of organic matter on earth.

carbuncle A large boil formed from the interconnection of several boils. Carbuncles cause severe pain associated with throbbing, possible fever, and a feeling of malaise.

carcinogen Any substance that promotes the formation of a cancerous growth.

carcinoma Any of the malignant cancerous growths of the cells that line organs.

cardiology The branch of medicine concerned with the study, diagnosis and treatment of the diseases and disorders of the heart.

cardiovascular system The complex network that

circulates blood to all the cells of the body. Food and oxygen are transported to each part of the body and waste products are removed through this system.

For more detailed information, see the ***FIRST AID GUIDE****, A Short Course in Anatomy (Circulatory System)* *and* ***FIRST AID GUIDE****, Shock (Nervous System).*

carpal tunnel syndrome Numbness, pain and weakness associated with compression of the *median nerve* at the wrist. The finger tendons and median nerve are contained in a tunnel formed by the carpal bones and sturdy membrane that stretches over them. Swelling of tissue within the tunnel can put pressure on the median nerve that controls the thumb, index finger, and middle finger.

Carpal tunnel syndrome may originate with pregnancy, a sprain or fracture of the wrist, arthritis, or any condition that tends to produce swelling or distortion of the wrist. The condition may be acquired or made worse by any activity that requires constant or repetitive twisting of the hand and wrist. Many cases are caused by long hours of working at a computer keyboard that requires maintaining the hands at an unnatural angle.

The pain resulting from the condition has been known to run up the arm, into the shoulder and even the neck. Eventually, the sufferer may be unable to make a fist as the fingers weaken and the muscles atrophy.

The first step to recovery is to alleviate the pressure on the nerve by removing the cause; in severe cases, surgery may be necessary to prevent permanent damage. In extreme cases, that is, where treatment has been delayed, full recovery may not be possible.

carrier An otherwise healthy individual who carries an infecting organism without evidence of symptoms, and who can infect others.

cartilage The tough connective tissue between bones. In

an embryo, cartilage forms the skeleton that is later changed into bone. In the adult, the cartilage serves primarily to reduce friction in the joints and also functions as a cushion.

catabolism The breaking down of complex substances by the body to provide energy; part of the total metabolic process. See also, ***anabolism***.

cataleptic One who suffers from periodic bouts of immobility typified by muscular rigidity, an apparent suspension of awareness and, sometimes, loss of consciousness.

cataphasia A condition characterized by frequent repetition of the same words or phrases.

cataract A cloudiness or haziness of the lens of the eye that degrades vision.

In normal vision, the lens of the eye is clear and serves to direct light into the eye. When the lens becomes more or less opaque, the light is diffused, blurring the vision.

To correct the condition, the defective lens may be surgically removed and replaced by an implant, special glasses, or contact lenses.

catatonia A phase of schizophrenia characterized by periods of muscular rigidity and withdrawal alternating with periods of agitation.

catheter A hollow tube inserted into the body for the injection or withdrawal of fluids.

cerebral palsy Any of a number of conditions marked by impaired muscle control.

Cerebral palsy is caused by nerve or brain damage, usually occurring around the time of birth. Early signs of the condition may be convulsions, partial paralysis of facial muscles, or slow development of motor functions, as sitting, crawling or standing. Later symptoms range from a simple lack of coordination to the inability to move normally. The damage that causes cerebral palsy may also cause a number of other conditions, such as mental retardation, or learning and behavioral disorders.

chemotherapy Treatment of disease with the use of chemicals.

chest The chest is formed by twenty–four ribs, twelve on each side, that are attached in the back to ***vertebrae***. The seven upper pairs of ribs are attached to the ***breastbone*** in front by ***cartilage***. The next three pairs of ribs are attached in front by a common cartilage to the seventh rib instead of the breastbone. The lower two pairs of ribs, known as the floating ribs, are not attached in front.

chest cavity The cavity is formed by the upper part of the spinal column or backbone at the back, ribs on the sides, and ribs and breastbone in front. The diaphragm separates the chest cavity and the abdominal cavity.

For a more detailed description, see the ***FIRST AID GUIDE**, A Short Course in Anatomy.*

chickenpox A highly contagious eruptive viral disease.

Chickenpox is so easily contracted that almost everyone is affected in childhood. The disease is spread by contact with an infected person or anything contaminated by an infected person. The virus that causes chickenpox is the same virus that causes shingles, and chicken pox may also be contracted from a person who has shingles.

Chickenpox usually appears as an itchy rash of small red spots around the trunk. The spots quickly develop into larger blisters that spread throughout the body. Within a few days, the blisters burst and form a crust.

With few exceptions, the greatest danger from chickenpox is the potential for infection or scarring from aggressive rubbing of the itching blisters. Children may need to wear mittens, especially at night, to keep from scratching.

Treatment consists mainly of alleviating symptoms, especially the annoying itch. Applications of a soothing lotion may help. Daily warm baths aid in clearing the rash and reduce the risk of infection. Aspirin should not be administered, because taking aspirin during a viral infection has been associated with bouts of ***Reye's syndrome***, a far more serious infection. Usually, one attack of chickenpox is enough to insure immunity for life.

chilblain Swelling of the skin due to exposure to cold. The condition is rare where heating and outdoor clothing are adequate to protect against cold and dampness.

Chilblains appear as itchy patches of red, swollen skin on the extremities that usually recede within a few days. A chronic condition can develop, however, with a discoloration of the skin accompanied by blisters that are painful and leave scars when they heal.

chill Shivering, and a sense of being cold, often associated with a sudden increase in body temperature.

A chill often heralds the onset of infection, caused by a temporary disorder of the nerve centers that regulate body temperature. Typically, the chill develops as fever rises and may recur intermittently until the fever breaks.

chiropody The science that deals with diseases, irregularities and injuries of the foot. See also, ***podiatry***.

cholera Any of various intestinal diseases transmitted in contaminated food or water, characterized by fever, vomiting, diarrhea, and dehydration.

cholesterol A component of animal fat, blood, nerve tissue, and bile, necessary to a healthy body, but that may be harmful in excess, as in formation of ***atherosclerosis***.

chromosomes The body of genetic material contained in the nucleus of a cell, the basic unit that makes up all living things. Chromosomes carry genes that transmit characteristics of a parent to a child, and through each cell throughout life, inasmuch as all cells in the body are created by division from the initial fertilized ovum, or egg.

cicatrix The fibrous tissue remaining after a wound has healed; a scar.

circadian rhythm The repetitive physiological processes of the body as they relate to the twenty–four hour cycle of the earth's rotation. Everyone has a so–called *internal clock* that maintains a cyclic pattern of body processes coinciding more or less with a twenty–four hour day, such as for the rising and falling of body temperature.

circulatory system The functions and organs that carry blood to and from all parts of the body.

For more detailed information, see the ***FIRST AID GUIDE**, A Short Course in Anatomy.*

cirrhosis Disease of the liver in which healthy cells are destroyed and replaced by fibrous tissue, the result of healing after sudden massive infection as by *acute hepatitis*, injury sustained over a period of months or years as by *chronic hepatitis* or blockage of the bile ducts, or of that created over a much longer period as by alcohol abuse, the most common cause of cirrhosis.

Treatment for the condition mainly involves correcting the cause, as by removing blockage or discontinuing ingestion of alcohol, then improving diet to accommodate the damaged liver, such as with large doses of vitamins and frequent small meals to reduce strain on the liver.

claudication Limping or lameness, especially that caused by restriction of the flow of blood to the leg muscles, such as by ***atherosclerosis.***

claustrophobia A morbid fear of being in a confined space or enclosed area.

cleft lip, cleft palate A birth defect in which a part or all of the upper structure of the mouth is split.

If not corrected, the deformity can cause difficulty with speech and hearing. The most immediate problem may be feeding—the infant with a cleft lip or palate may not be able to suckle. Often a special device or an appliance can be used to facilitate feeding until the time considered suitable by the physician to attempt corrective surgery.

clot See ***blood clot***

clubfoot A birth defect in which the foot is turned inward or otherwise twisted.

Early correction may involve manipulation and the use of casts or other devices to gradually correct the position of the foot. Some surgery may be required to lengthen the Achilles tendon or correct the ankle joint. If early attempts at correction are not successful, or not undertaken, extensive surgery may be required later.

coagulation The transformation of a liquid into a soft, congealed mass, as in clotting.

cocaine A narcotic used as a local anesthetic, effective when applied to mucous membrane, that is addictive when inhaled. See also, ***codeine.***

coccyx A small bone that forms the lower extremity of the spinal column.

codeine An opium derivative, used for the relief of pain, similar to morphine, but not as addictive.

cod-liver oil Fish oil that is rich in vitamins A and D, often taken as a dietary supplement.

cold sore A viral infection that causes small blisters to appear about the area of the mouth, usually following an illness accompanied by fever.

colostomy A surgical procedure opening the wall of the abdomen and joining it to an opening in the large intestine to allow the elimination of body waste.

A colostomy may be created to correct a condition caused by obstruction or disease. Waste discharged through the opening is collected in a disposable bag. Once the diet is properly regulated, the colostomy causes little restriction of normal activities.

compress A pad, often of cloth, used to apply heat, moisture, or medication.

compulsion An irresistible desire, often irrational and repetitive, to do something.

concretion A hard, inorganic mass in the body, as a kidney stone; a ***calculus***.

concussion An injury to the brain caused by sudden shock, as a sharp blow to the head.

A simple concussion, brought about by the brain striking the inside of the skull, that may bruise brain tissue, cause bleeding inside the skull, and loss of consciousness.

Unconsciousness may last a few minutes or a few hours; a longer period usually indicates more serious damage. Other symptoms of a concussion are feelings of nausea, dizziness, and headache that may last for several days. There may also be a loss of memory covering a period just prior to the injury until several hours after.

Any signs of more serious injury, as an open wound, partial paralysis anywhere in the body, or sharply dilated pupils should be referred to a physician.

Normally, rest is all that is required for recuperation: relax, avoid any medication stronger than aspirin and, if vomiting occurs, avoid solid food. Sleep should be postponed for several hours to be certain that no unusual symptoms arise; once allowed to sleep, the victim should be awakened every two hours to give his or her name and location to confirm that there are no complications.

Consult a physician if a headache grows more severe, vision becomes blurred, or there is any other abnormality of the eyes, and in cases of spasms or staggering.

congenital Existing from birth; descriptive of a condition present at birth and that is not hereditary.

congestion An abnormal accumulation of body fluid, especially one that tends to clog, as the nasal passages.

conjunctivitis Inflammation of the conjunctiva, the membrane that covers the eyeball and lines the inner surface of the eyelid. Conjunctivitis is often caused by invasion of microorganisms and may be contracted by dust, smoke, or chemicals.

The condition is characterized by redness of the eye, burning or itching, and a sensitivity to light. There is often periodic tearing and a discharge of pus. Treatment varies with the cause and its severity. The eye should be rested and protected from bright light as much as possible; if eyelids are held closed by dry discharge, it can be softened by gentle bathing in warm water. Care should be taken to isolate handkerchiefs, towels, etc. used by the subject, as conjunctivitis is highly contagious.

connective tissue Fibrous tissue that serves to connect the cells and support the organs of the body.

contact dermatitis An inflammation of the skin caused by direct contact with an irritant which may cause redness, swelling, blistering, burning, itching, or tenderness in the area of contact.

Contact dermatitis may be caused by any of a number of substances, such as hair coloring, cosmetics, household cleaners, or by plants, such as poison ivy and poison oak. Identifying the offending substance may be a simple process of elimination or it may require testing for allergies. The infection may clear when the substance is avoided; severe cases should be referred to a doctor.

contagion The spread of disease, directly or indirectly, from one person to another.

contaminated Descriptive of that which is unclean, often in reference to food or water infected by bacteria.

contusion A bruise or injury that does not break the skin.

convulsion Sudden, involuntary contractions or spasms of the muscles.

coronary bypass See ***bypass***

corticosteroids Any of the hormones produced in the cortex of the adrenal glands. More than 30 corticosteroids regulate essential processes in the body. One group, the *mineralocorticoids*, help maintain the salt and water balance in the body. A second group, the *glucocorticoids*, help regulate the use of sugars and proteins. The third group, *androgens*, stimulate the development of secondary male sex characteristics.

cough Sudden, noisy expulsion of air from the lungs.
A defensive reflex that clears the lungs of excess mucus or irritating matter, the cough will persist as long as the condition that causes it, but it may be suppressed by soothing liquids or drugs that act on the cough reflex.

CPR CardioPulmonary Resuscitation; the use of artificial ventilation, that is, mouth–to–mouth breathing and external heart compression, or rhythmic pressure on the breastbone, to revive one who has suffered cardiac arrest.

cretinism A severe congenital thyroid deficiency. The infant suffering from cretinism exhibits retarded physical and mental development that, if diagnosed early, may be treated and cured.

crib death SIDS, *sudden infant death syndrome*. The sudden mysterious death of an apparently healthy infant.

croup An inflammation of the larynx.
Mostly confined to children, the croup causes swelling of the larynx, or voice box, so that breathing becomes difficult. A characteristic barking cough is the result of air forced through the swollen larynx. Breathing may be further impaired if mucus blocks the windpipe and bronchi that connect to the lungs. Immediate medical attention is critical, because swelling may close off the breathing passage completely. Meanwhile, calm the child—an attack of croup is frightening and fear makes the symptoms

worse. Sit in a bathroom with the hot shower running—warm, moist air should ease the symptoms. Good results may be realized with a humidifier or by breathing over a container of hot water; however, resting in a parent's arms in the steamy bathroom is probably most soothing.

cyst An abnormal sac containing liquid or semiliquid waste material. Cysts often do not cause symptoms and are therefore not treated; one that causes pressure or other problems may be surgically removed.

decortication Removal of the outer layer of an organ.

defibrillation A technique to correct fibrillation, an abnormal heartbeat commonly caused by a heart attack, when part of the heart quivers or acts independently of the normal heartbeat. The heart is not then able to pump blood through the body and death will result if the condition is not corrected. Protracted exposure to the cold or a severe electrical shock can also cause fibrillation.

dehydration Loss of water from the body; condition produced by loss or deprivation of water from body tissue.

Dehydration may be caused by the inability to take in water due to illness or disease, or by loss of water from vomiting, diarrhea, uncontrolled secretion of urine, or excessive sweating. A serious side affect of dehydration is the critical loss of salt from the body. Unchecked, dehydration may result in death in a matter of days.

delirium A temporary mental disorder characterized by excitement, confusion, and hallucinations.

Delirium may be brought on by any of a number of traumatic conditions, as by infection, drugs, withdrawal of certain drugs or alcohol, high fever, etc.

Condition of the subject may undergo abrupt radical change with varying frequency, as from a state of agitated restlessness to one of serenity and comprehension.

delirium tremens DT's; disordered perception brought

on by trauma associated with alcoholism.

Delirium tremens may be triggered by excessive alcohol consumption, by the consumption of alcohol in conjunction with other drugs, or by withdrawal of alcohol after a period of regular excessive consumption.

The victim may suffer distinctive tremors, frightening hallucinations, rapid pulse, periods of profuse sweating, an overwhelming feeling of terror, and extreme agitation.

delusion A belief maintained in spite of irrefutable evidence to the contrary. Delusion may be part of a psychotic episode in which perception is altered to cause irrational interpretation of an ordinary event.

On another level, delusion may be formed from hallucination or an elaborate scheme of rationalization that, although connected, has no basis in reality. Delusion may also be related to depression, as in feelings of hypochondria or guilt, where negative feelings relate to personal condition, fortunes, or worthiness not supported in fact.

dementia Mental impairment or deficiency caused by injury or disease that may be associated with senility, ***Alzheimer's disease***, a blood clot or tumor of the brain, etc. A loss of memory, especially for recent events, is the most common symptom. The condition can progress to severe degradation or total destruction of intellectual powers, deprivation of emotional control, and a complete personality transformation. See also, ***amentia***.

dentistry The work of one whose profession is the care of the teeth and the surrounding tissue; the diagnosis and treatment of the diseases and disorders of the mouth as well as prevention of those conditions.

Routine care is normally provided by a general practitioner qualified to recommend a specialist if one is needed. Among the specialized fields of dentistry are: *orthodontia,* concerned with straightening of teeth; *periodontia,* that deals with diseases of the gums; *prosthodontia,* the replacement of missing teeth; *endodontia,* focusing on diseases of the pulp and root canal surgery; and *exodontia,* dealing with the extraction of teeth.

dermatitis Inflammation of the skin caused by any of a number of substances, such as hair coloring, cosmetics, or household cleaners; by plants, such as poison ivy or poison oak; or by ingesting certain foods or medications. Some forms of dermatitis are a secondary symptom of diseases affecting other parts of the body. Others, such as *exfoliative dermatitis* that causes the shedding of skin and hair should be referred to a physician for proper diagnosis and cure. See also, ***Contact Dermatitis***.

dermatology The study of diseases and disorders of the skin. Because of the relationship between diseases of the skin and allergies or other diseases (see ***dermatitis***), the dermatologist must have a thorough knowledge of diseases that relate to dermatitis and to allergies.

diabetes mellitus A condition in which the body is not able to satisfactorily process ingested sugar.
For more detailed information, see the ***FIRST AID GUIDE,*** *Medical Emergencies.*

diabetic coma A state of stupor or lethargy leading to coma, brought on by an inadequate supply of insulin.
For more detailed information, see the ***FIRST AID GUIDE,*** *Medical Emergencies.*

diagnosis The process of identifying a disease by careful examination of symptoms.

dialysis The process of removing waste matter and maintaining the electrolyte balance of the blood by diffusion. Normally, dialysis is performed by the kidneys. One who suffers kidney failure, temporary or permanent, must have the blood cleansed by an artificial kidney machine. In the artificial kidney or dialysis machine, blood from a tube implanted in an artery is circulated through the apparatus where it contacts a thin membrane that separates the blood from a solution containing a precise concentration of electrolytes. By the process of osmosis (the tendency of fluid to diffuse through a membrane from a stronger to a weaker solution) waste is passed through the membrane to the solution and electrolytes are passed from the solution to the blood.

The blood cells, too large to pass through the membrane, are not affected and the revitalized blood is returned to the subject's body through a tube implanted in a vein.

diaphragm The muscular partition in the body that separates the chest cavity and the abdominal cavity.

digestion The process of breaking down food into substances that can be used by the body and those that are to be discharged as waste.

Digestion begins in the mouth where food is ground by the teeth and mixed with saliva. The saliva moistens food for easier passage and begins the breakdown of starches.

Food is passed down the throat through the esophagus and into the stomach, where it is combined with digestive juices to partly liquefy it for passage into the small intestine. In the duodenum, the first section of the small intestine, bile from the liver aids in the absorption of fat; digestive juices from the pancreas further facilitate the digestion and absorption of food. Anything not absorbed into the bloodstream from the small intestine is passed on to the large intestine for discharge from the body.

diphtheria An acute, highly contagious disease that affects the tonsils, airways and larynx.

Diphtheria bacteria destroy the outer layer of mucous membrane in the throat or larynx. The principal mark of the disease is a grayish membrane over the throat formed from dead cells, bacteria, etc.

Diphtheria is transmitted by drops of moisture from the nose and throat of an infected person, often a carrier who is not aware of the presence of the disease. Symptoms of the disease include sore throat, hoarseness, a rasping cough and fever. Children may be nauseous, with chills and a headache. The characteristic membrane may vary in color or not appear at all; however, if it does form, it may detach and block off the victim's air supply. The disease may be complicated by inflammation of the heart muscles or nerves. Because of the danger of suffocation, victims need to be hospitalized where they can recuperate under close supervision.

dislocation A twisting out of normal position, as a bone. For more detailed information, see the ***FIRST AID GUIDE****, Sprains, Strains, and Fractures.*

diverticulosis, diverticulitis A *diverticulum* is a small sac or pouch; *diverticulosis* is the existence of *diverticula* (plural form of *diverticulum*) on the wall of the bowel.; *diverticulitis* is an inflammation of the *diverticula*.

It is possible, though not proven, that diverticula are formed when a lack of roughage in the diet causes the muscle layer in the wall of the colon to overwork or when those muscles are weakened by age, so that pressure in the colon forces the intestinal lining through the weak spots in the wall. Generally, diverticulosis exhibits no symptoms; however, waste matter may become trapped in diverticula and reduce the flow of blood to the walls, paving the way for diverticulitis.

In addition to discomfort and pain in the abdomen, diverticulitis may lead to the formation of a fistula, or unnatural channel, between the colon and the bladder or another organ, infecting it as well.

DNA, RNA *DNA* is deoxyribonucleic acid, the basic component of living tissue that holds genetic information to insure inheritance and transmission of chromosomes and genes. *RNA* is ribonucleic acid, that carries genetic information from DNA for synthesis of protein in the cell.

DT's See ***delirium tremens***

duodenal ulcer An ulcer or open sore affecting the duodenum, the first section of the small intestine.

A *peptic ulcer* is an infection in any part of the digestive tract exposed to pepsin, a digestive juice. A *duodenal ulcer* is a peptic ulcer occurring in the duodenum when its lining is attacked by digestive juices to which it is normally impervious. Though unconfirmed, the cause of the ulcer may be excessive secretions of digestive juices brought about by certain types of diet or medication.

The ulcer may remain undetected for lack of symptoms, but usually will cause some discomfort, such as a burning sensation within an hour of two of eating.

The presence of an ulcer needs to be confirmed by a physician who can prescribe medication, but treatment may simply require avoiding foods that cause distress as well as those that stimulate the secretion of digestive fluids, such as caffeinated beverages and alcohol

dysentery An inflammation of the colon characterized by pain, cramps and diarrhea caused by bacteria *(bacillary dysentery)* or amoebae *(amoebic dysentery)* spread through poor hygiene, as by contaminated food.

dyslexia Any of a number of reading, writing or learning disorders in one who is otherwise of normal intelligence.

Most symptoms relate to a lack of directional or positional sense in that letters in a word or words may be read or written out of their normal order, or there may be difficulty matching names with their respective images.

dyspepsia Indigestion; impaired digestion.

Belching, stomach pains, a feeling that the stomach is overfull, sour taste, and even nausea, are all signs of indigestion, usually brought about by poor dietary habits. Ingesting fatty foods, rich foods, spicy foods, an excess of alcohol, or irregular meals make one a prime candidate for dyspepsia. Dyspepsia is quite common and seldom causes more than temporary discomfort; however, if it is chronic it may be warning of a more serious condition.

eczema Any inflammatory disease of the skin.
Eczema may be redness, burning or itching, blistering, the discharge of serous matter, and crusts or scabs.

edema Swelling caused by the accumulation of fluid in tissues or a body cavity.

embolism Blockage of a blood vessel by an obstruction called an *embolus*. A common form of embolus is a blood clot or plaque from a clogged artery or heart valve. An air embolus may develop if excessive air is admitted during an intravenous injection, during surgery, or in moving between an area of high pressure and one of lower pressure (see ***bends***).
An embolism reduces the blood to the area where it occurs causing tissue damage. Discomfort or pain may be the main symptom of an embolism with others depending on the location, such as an embolism in a brain artery that emulates the symptoms of a ***stroke***.

emphysema A condition in which air spaces in the lungs are enlarged. Emphysema often develops from inflammation, swelling and excessive mucus production associated with bronchitis or other diseases that trap air in the lungs. The result is a loss of effectiveness in moving air in and out of the lungs, putting extra strain on the heart.
Emphysema is characterized by shortness of breath. Difficulty in breathing may be accompanied by a persisting, painful cough. Sufferers of emphysema tire quite easily, largely a result of energy required just to get enough air.

encephalitis Inflammation of the brain.

Encephalitis may be caused by bacteria or parasites, but most commonly is the result of a virus, either as a direct effect or a complication from an infection. Some of the viruses are carried by mosquitoes while others are associated with childhood diseases, as measles, mumps, or chicken pox—children are the main victims.

endocarditis Inflammation of the valves or lining of the heart.

endocrinology Study of the endocrine system and its functions, and the diagnosis and treatment of disorders. The endocrine system is comprised of the glands that secrete vital hormones into the bloodstream, including the pituitary, adrenal, thyroid, pancreas, ovaries, and testes. The hormones secreted by these glands travel throughout the body to control and combine a number of body functions. Growth abnormalities, diabetes and other diseases may be attributed to disorders of the endocrine system.

enteritis Inflammation of the intestinal tract. Enteritis is most commonly found as a bacterial or viral infection in the small intestine as the result of the consumption of contaminated food or water.

epidemiology The study of the communication of disease in general, the relationship between certain diseases and the conditions under which they flourish, and means of prevention, such as vaccines. The epidemiologist is also concerned with non–infectious diseases that are widespread or of questionable origin, such as the relationship between certain illnesses and environmental pollution, or toxic substances in foods or other products.

epilepsy A neurological disorder that causes recurring seizures. Commonly, epilepsy has no apparent cause, although in some cases it may be traced to a source, such as a tumor that forms pressure on the brain, an injury to the brain, or disorder caused by drugs. Epilepsy cannot

be prevented, but the seizures may be controlled by medication, allowing the epileptic to lead a normal life.
For more information, see the ***FIRST AID GUIDE****, Medical Emergencies.*

esophagus The food pipe that extends from the throat, through the chest, and ends at the stomach.

excretory systems Those parts of the body concerned with the separation and elimination of waste products.
For a more detailed description, see the ***FIRST AID GUIDE****, A Short Course in Anatomy.*

extrasystole An abnormal contraction of the heart.
Normally, the heart beats in a regular rhythm; an extrasystole is a contraction of the heart caused by a signal emanating from somewhere other than the heart's natural pacemaker. The extrasystole may be detected as a skip, flutter, or extra beat. It may be experienced periodically, triggered by stress or excitement, or it may be recurring, as a symptom of heart disease or reaction to drugs.
Whether or not the extrasystole is a matter for concern depends on its cause, frequency, and the general health of the subject. Prolonged or repeated recurrence should be referred to a physician.

extremities Descriptive of arms and legs including their joining to the trunk of the body.
For more detailed information, see the ***FIRST AID GUIDE****, A Short Course in Anatomy.*

febrile Descriptive of body temperature that is above normal; feverish.

fever blisters An eruption about the mouth accompanying a cold or fever; a cold sore or *herpes simplex*.

fistula An abnormal duct or passageway in the body. A fistula may be congenital or it may be the result of complications from an infection.

food allergy Excessive sensitivity to a particular food that is otherwise considered safe to eat.

The foods that most commonly trigger an immune system reaction are dairy products, seafood, chocolate, tomatoes, strawberries, and citrus fruits. A food reaction is usually manifested by digestive disorder, as cramps, nausea, vomiting, or diarrhea; hives, rash, nasal congestion, headache, or ***anaphylactic shock*** may also be symptoms.

When food allergy is suspected, the offending substance can often be pinpointed by process of elimination, sampling or excluding foods one at a time to determine if symptoms recur. It is prudent to maintain a record of all foods eaten during this time as reaction or lack of reaction may be the result of certain foods in combination.

food poisoning Acute distress caused by food containing toxins or bacteria. The subsistence may be one that contains poison in its natural state, as certain wild mushrooms and plants, or one that has been contaminated, as food that has been improperly stored.

Cramps, diarrhea and vomiting are most commonly associated with food poisoning, but symptoms may be more severe, causing difficulty in breathing, blurred vision or paralysis. Any symptoms that are excessive or that persevere should be treated by a physician.

fracture Any break or crack in a bone.

Any suspected fracture should be referred to a physician, as improper healing can have serious consequences.

For more detailed information, see the ***FIRST AID GUIDE***, *Sprains, Strains, and Fractures.*

friable Of that which is easily pulverized.

frostbite Tissue damage caused by extreme cold.

For more information about symptoms and treatment, see the ***FIRST AID GUIDE***, *Environmental Emergencies.*

fulminating Of the rapid and severe onset of a disease.

furuncle See ***boil***

gallstones Hardened masses formed in the gallbladder or in the bile duct leading from the gallbladder to the small intestine. Formed from cholesterol, blood, bile, and other substances, gallstones can cause pain in the abdomen, indigestion, especially after eating fatty foods, or nausea.
Sometimes the stones pass into the intestine and are excreted. If the stones become trapped in the bile duct, the pain is much more severe and may be accompanied by chills, fever, vomiting and jaundice, especially if the flow of bile is blocked.

gangrene Death of body tissue, usually caused by a reduction or complete absence of blood to a section of the tissue, although bacterial infection that destroys tissue may play a critical part in its formation.
Gangrene may be the result of burns, freezing, physical injury, a blood clot, bacteria or any other condition that interferes with the flow of blood and destroys tissue.

gastroenteritis Inflammation of the lining of the stomach and intestines, often the result of infection by bacteria or virus, but also be caused by reaction to certain foods or drugs, food poisoning, or over–consumption of alcohol.
The onset of gastroenteritis may be signaled by discomfort in the abdomen, gas pains, cramps, nausea or diarrhea. Usually all that is required to alleviate the symptoms is rest, plenty of liquids and a temporary bland diet. Medical care may be required if symptoms persist in order to rule out a more serious condition. Excessive vomiting and diarrhea that may lead to dehydration also requires medical attention, especially for infants.

gastroenterology The branch of medicine that deals with the study, diagnosis and treatment of diseases and disorders of the stomach and intestines.

gene Any of the units that occur in the chromosome and carry the traits that are passed on from parent to child

generic Of a class or group—descriptive of drugs and other products prescribed and sold by their scientific name, less expensive than one sold by a brand name.

genetic Descriptive of characteristics that may be inherited; distinctive from *congenital*, dating from birth.

genetic disorder A disease or malformation that may be passed from one generation to another.

In some cases, a link is clearly established, as a condition associated with a particular chromosome; in others, association is by observation, as the tendency of a particular condition to occur in succeeding generations.

germ Generally, a reference to microorganisms, especially bacteria, that are capable of producing disease.

German measles A mild, contagious, viral infection; *rubella*. The most serious problem associated with German measles is the likelihood of birth defects when the virus has been contracted during pregnancy.

gerontology The study of the aging process and the diseases and disabilities associated with it.

gingivitis Inflammation of the gums.

Gingivitis is usually due to a combination of poor diet and poor dental hygiene, although it may be caused by vitamin deficiency or as a complication of a disease.

The discomfort and minor bleeding associated with gingivitis may be alleviated by reducing intake of sugar and alcohol, increasing intake of vitamin C, and improving dental hygiene. In some cases, it is necessary for a dental surgeon to cut away damaged portions of the gum.

gland Any organ that secretes a substance to be used elsewhere in the body.

glaucoma A disorder of the eye caused by increased pressure within the eyeball.

Normally fluid in the eyeball is under slight pressure carefully regulated by the body. When fluid fails to drain and maintain constant pressure, the buildup causes damage to the structure. Glaucoma may be linked to other diseases of the eye or to the use of certain drugs.

Acute glaucoma is rare. The symptoms are so intense as to be impossible to ignore: extreme pain and a sudden blurring of vision. Deterioration by chronic glaucoma, on the other hand, is free of pain and so very gradual that it may go unnoticed for a long time. There may be some loss of peripheral vision without other symptoms, followed by blurred vision, difficulty in adjusting to bright lights or darkness, and slight pain around the eye, symptoms that may be sporadic. Most eye examinations include a check for glaucoma in order to catch it in the early stages when it can be treated most effectively.

globulin Any of several simple proteins that comprise one of the two major protein groups of the blood that are insoluble in water. See also, ***albumin***.

glossitis Inflammation of the tongue that may be specific, as from an injury to the tongue, or symptomatic of another disorder, as of a disease or vitamin deficiency.

The symptoms of glossitis vary considerably, depending on the cause. Some of the manifestations are redness, swelling, white patches, and ulcers. Severe acute glossitis produced by infection, burns, or injury can bring about pain and swelling that causes the tongue to project into the throat, obstructing the airway. In severe cases, chewing, swallowing, or speaking may be impaired.

glucose A form of sugar found naturally in honey, fruit, and in the blood.

glycemia The presence of sugar in the blood. See also, ***hyperglycemia, hypoglycemia.***

glycogen A form of carbohydrate, found mainly in the muscles and in the liver, that is changed into glucose to meet the body's demands.

goiter Enlargement of the thyroid gland that appears as a swelling at the side or front of the neck.

Goiter may be caused by a diet deficient in iodine necessary for the production of thyroid hormone or by an excess of foods that inhibit production of thyroid hormone, as cabbage or soya. Often the cause is unknown. Swelling is the result of a futile attempt by the gland to produce more hormone by enlarging cells within the gland.

gout Inflammation of a joint caused by excess uric acid in the bloodstream. Gout is the result of the body's inability to properly process uric acid, a chemical normally found in the blood and urine. Excess uric acid may crystallize and be deposited in the skin, joints and kidneys.

An attack of gout is the body's response to the crystal deposits. The initial attack is usually concentrated in a single joint; subsequent attacks may involve several joints. Attacks are very painful and the area becomes extremely sensitive, followed by redness, warmth and swelling.

A physician should be consulted for treatment, even when the symptoms disappear within a day or two, because the condition tends to reappear with attacks of increasing frequency, duration, and severity.

graft Living tissue that is taken from a body to be surgically implanted in another part of the body or in another body. See also, ***transplant.***

gynecology The branch of medicine concerned with the diagnosis and treatment of disorders of the female reproductive system.

hallucination A false sense of perception.

A hallucination can affect the senses of sight, hearing, taste, or smell, manifested in something as simple as a flash of light to a detailed and clearly identifiable sight or sound. Hallucinations may be symptomatic of a mental disorder or the result of physical illness. Recurring and often terrifying hallucinations may accompany high fever, alcoholism, drug abuse or severe injury. Disease or a tumor of the brain may cause hallucinations related to a particular sense depending on the area affected.

hay fever A short–lived, seasonal, allergic reaction to the pollen of a particular plant or group of plants manifested by cold–like symptoms; *pollinosis*.

Common symptoms include itchy watery eyes, sneezing, watery discharge from the nose, headache, irritability, tiredness, insomnia, coughing, and wheezing. Over–the–counter remedies are available to the sufferer including antihistamines that counteract histamine released by the body in reaction to the allergen, corticosteroids that reduce inflammation, and eye drops to relieve itching and redness. Severe cases may warrant consultation with a physician who can prescribe desensitization shots that induce the body to develop a tolerance to the allergen.

head The upper part of the human body, housing the brain and organs for sight, hearing, smell and taste, joined to the trunk by the neck. The head is composed of twenty–two bones, eight that are closely united to form the skull, a bony case that encloses and protects the brain, and fourteen other bones that form the face. The only movable joint in the head is the lower jaw.

heart A hollow, muscular organ about the size of a fist lying in the lower central region of the chest cavity that keeps blood under pressure and in constant circulation throughout the body.

For more information, see the ***FIRST AID GUIDE,*** *A Short Course in Anatomy (Circulatory System).*

heart attack A sudden diminishing of the heart's ability to function; *myocardial infarction*. A heart attack occurs when the oxygen–rich blood supply to the heart is cut off by damage or blockage to the coronary artery.

For additional information, see the ***FIRST AID GUIDE,*** *Artificial Ventilation.*

heart murmur An abnormal heart sound that can usually be detected only with the aid of a stethoscope.

Generally, heart murmurs are harmless, but can be early indicators of heart disease or a structural abnormality, such as a hole in the wall between the chambers of the heart, or incomplete closure or obstruction of a valve. A heart murmur may be congenital, or the result of disease.

heat cramps Cramps caused by a critical loss of salt.

For more detailed information, see the ***FIRST AID GUIDE,*** *Environmental Emergencies.*

heat exhaustion A condition caused by prolonged exposure to a hot environment.

For more detailed information, see the ***FIRST AID GUIDE,*** *Environmental Emergencies.*

heat stroke A state of collapse brought on by exposure to heat; sunstroke.

For more information about causes and symptoms, see the ***FIRST AID GUIDE,*** *Environmental Emergencies.*

hematemesis Vomiting of blood. Hematemesis may be caused by a simple irritation of the stomach, as by aspirin or overindulgence in alcohol, or it may be an indication of more serious illness, such as ulcers or cancer.

hematology The study of blood, blood–forming organs, and related diseases. Hematology is concerned with diagnostic techniques for exploring disease processes through examination of blood and bone marrow samples, as well as the workings, disorders and diseases of the blood and blood–forming organs themselves

hematoma A swelling make up of blood, usually clotted; a bruise; usually the direct result of trauma, although the blood may come from a vessel that is fragile or damaged. Most hematomas heal without treatment, but there is a

danger of infection, especially from a bruise around the nose or eyes. Unusual behavior or complaint of headaches after an injury should be referred to a physician.
In cases of severe trauma, internal hematomas may develop. These too, will usually heal without treatment, although injuries to the head carry the possibility of belated symptoms of headache, drowsiness or paralysis that signal more serious injury that must be treated quickly.

hemoglobin The substance in red blood cells that enables them to carry oxygen and gives them their color.

hemophilia A hereditary disease in which improper clotting puts the sufferer in danger of a severe loss of blood from a minor cut or injury.

hemorrhage The escape of blood from an artery, vein or capillary. *Hemorrhage* often implies a considerable loss of blood or uncontrolled bleeding.
Normally, when blood vessels are torn or broken, the blood quickly forms clots, stemming the flow; however, when serious injury or disease, such as hemophilia, peptic ulcer, or cancer is involved, the body's normal clotting mechanism may malfunction or prove inadequate.
The seriousness of hemorrhage depends on the location and amount of bleeding. Severe hemorrhage may cause rapid pulse, dizziness, a drop in blood pressure, a rise in pulse rate, and clammy or sweaty skin. Blood in the stool, urine, or vomitus may indicate internal bleeding and should be reported immediately to a physician.

hepatitis Inflammation of the liver, usually referring to one of a number of viral infections, characterized by jaundice. Most common are hepatitis A or *infectious hepatitis* and hepatitis B or *serum hepatitis*.
Hepatitis A is transmitted through contaminated food, water, or contact with the stool of an infected person. The infection may be so mild as to be without symptoms,

although the infection can still be passed on to others. Hepatitis B virus enters the bloodstream through contact with contaminated blood or other body fluids such as saliva, semen, urine, or tears; thus, it may be transmitted by sexual contact or, infrequently, by casual contact. Hepatitis may cause fatigue, joint and muscle pain, loss of appetite, nausea, vomiting, and diarrhea or constipation, accompanied by a low grade fever. As the disease progresses, the liver may enlarge and become tender. The characteristic jaundice is caused by accumulation of bile pigment in the blood that turns skin and whites of the eyes yellow. The disappearance of jaundice generally signals the start of recovery from hepatitis A; the hepatitis B virus, however, may persist for years or even a lifetime. Any suspicion of hepatitis infection requires medical attention to avoid permanent liver damage. Although there is no cure, the physician can recommend a diet and life style that will minimize strain on the liver.

heredity The transmission of characteristics from parent to offspring. Each characteristic is conveyed by a gene, the primary unit of heredity. Genes are arranged on chromosomes in a precise order and every human cell is comprised of forty–six chromosomes arranged in twenty–three pairs. On inception, each of the two chromosomes that are to be joined split in half and reunite with the corresponding half of its counterpart; thus, half of the chromosomes that will make up a unique new individual is contributed by each parent. It is this pairing of chromosomes and the genes they carry that determine the characteristics of the offspring.

hernia The protrusion of a body part through a defect in the wall that surrounds it. A hernia may be congenital, or it may develop when muscle walls are weakened by strain or disease.

herpes Any of a number of acute viral infections that are characterized by clusters of small blisters on the skin or mucous membrane. *Herpes simplex* is a recurring form of herpes that usually affects the area around the mouth or the genitals. *Herpes zoster*, see ***shingles.***

hiatal hernia The protrusion of the stomach above the diaphragm; a *hiatus* or *diaphragmatic hernia*.

The diaphragm divides the chest cavity and the abdominal cavity. Normally, the esophagus passes through the diaphragm and connects to the stomach below. A hiatal hernia occurs when a portion of the stomach protrudes up into the chest cavity through the passageway in the diaphragm used by the esophagus.

hiccup, hiccough A sudden intake of air checked by closure of the glottis causing a typical sound.

The hiccup originates with irritation to the phrenic nerve, usually caused by eating or drinking too fast. This causes an involuntary spasm of the muscle of the diaphragm. The spasm causes a sharp intake of air stopped by sudden closing of the glottis at the back of the throat. This sudden stop produces the characteristic jerk and sound. Unless an attack persists, the hiccup is of little significance. Although cures for hiccups abound, some rather bizarre, most effective is holding the breath for as long as possible so as to suppress the response of the diaphragm.

hirsutism Growth of hair that is excessive or that appears in unusual areas.

hives An allergic condition characterized by itchy blotches or welts; *urticaria*.

Hives may be caused by allergens in food, as tomatoes or strawberries; certain drugs; bacteria; animal hair; or the environment, as exposure to cold or the sun. An outbreak of hives may last less than an hour or continue for weeks, often subsiding, then reappearing. A mild attack is merely annoying, but more serious attacks may be accompanied by fever or nausea and even difficulty in breathing if the respiratory tract is infected. Treatment generally involves administering antihistamines.

Hodgkin's disease A malignant disease of the lymphatic system; a type of lymphoma. The cancer tends to attack lymph glands throughout the body and often spreads to neighboring organs.

hormone A substance secreted by a gland and that is carried elsewhere to influence the function of specific cells or organs.

host Any living thing, such as a person, animal, plant, or organ, that offers a suitable environment to shelter a parasite, infection, etc.

hydrophobia See ***rabies***

hyperglycemia An excess of sugar in the blood, as in ***diabetes mellitus.***

hypertension High blood pressure.

Blood flowing through the arteries under higher than normal pressure places stress on the artery walls that can damage them and interfere with the blood supply to vital organs, causing heart attack, kidney failure, or stroke.

Hypertension exhibits no distinctive symptoms: headache, fatigue, dizziness, ringing in the ears, frequent nosebleeds, etc. caused by high blood pressure are all symptoms that may be attributable to other causes.

To test for hypertension, a physician checks the blood pressure using a ***sphygmomanometer***, a device with an inflatable cuff that is wrapped around the subject's arm and that has a gauge to indicate pressure.

Hypertension responds well to treatment; a minor variation from normal may simply require a change in lifestyle: weight loss, reduction of stress, a program of regular exercise, and a limitation of the intake of sodium. For more severe cases, medication may be prescribed.

hyperthyroidism Any of the disorders that involve overactivity of the thyroid gland. The output of thyroid hormone is regulated by the thyroid gland's reaction to thyroid–stimulating hormone produced in the pituitary gland when thyroid hormone is needed. Hyperthyroidism occurs when the thyroid is no longer sensitive to this regulating mechanism: thyroid hormone is produced even in the absence of thyroid–stimulating hormone.

Thyroid hormone is involved in a number of processes throughout the body, such as regulation of body temperature, growth, fertility, and the conversion of food to energy. Such involvement portends a variety of symptoms, such as overheating, weight loss coupled with increased appetite, a reduction or cessation of menstruation, rapid heartbeat, hyperactivity, and tremors.

Hyperthyroidism can be treated with a variety of medications, depending on the severity of the condition.

hyperventilation Abnormally rapid or deep breathing, causing excessive loss of carbon dioxide that can make one light–headed, or cause loss of consciousness.

hypnosis A passive state induced by suggestion.

A hypnotic state is brought about by having a subject in a quiet environment concentrate while a hypnotist quietly urges acceptance of the receptive state of mind.

Although not everyone can be hypnotized, and hypnotism is not often encountered in orthodox medicine, it has been successfully used in the suppression of pain, of certain symptoms, and the altering of harmful lifestyle patterns, such as smoking.

hypoallergenic Descriptive of anything that is less likely than another similar product to cause an allergic reaction, often claimed of certain soaps and cosmetics.

hypochondria Abnormal preoccupation with one's

health. Hypochondria may be a concern for health in general, imagining symptoms that change from time to time, usually after assurance by a physician that nothing is wrong, or obsession with a particular ailment or disease, or the condition of a specific organ.

hypoglycemia An abnormal lack of sugar in the blood.

Normally, during digestion, insulin secreted by the pancreas reduces the level of blood sugar, called glucose, by enabling the body cells to absorb it. *Reactive hypoglycemia* is triggered by the ingestion of food and occurs when too much insulin is secreted during digestion causing the cells to overabsorb sugar from the blood. *Fasting hypoglycemia* is caused by inadequate conversion of carbohydrates into glucose, overabsorption of glucose by the body, or an insulin producing tumor that does not respond to normal stimuli. At risk from fasting hypoglycemia are heavy drinkers whose sugar storage and release system in the liver is upset by alcohol or those who have not eaten for an extended period

Either type of hypoglycemia can cause fatigue, nervousness, inability to concentrate, dizziness, confusion, headache, hunger pangs, or visual impairment.

hypotension Unusually low blood pressure.

Although high blood pressure can be a serious problem that leads to complications, in most cases low blood pressure is not threatening nor does it require treatment.

It is normal for blood pressure to vary, depending on factors such as age, sex, etc. Infrequently, a medical problem, such as certain types of heart disease, cause low blood pressure; in such cases, treatment of the condition corrects the hypotension. One recurring symptom of hypotension may be that of dizziness when rising quickly from a sitting or reclining position. Normally, when such a move is made, blood vessels contract to prevent a sudden loss of blood to the brain; however, for the sufferer of hypotension, this mechanism may not work properly, and he or she may find it necessary to rise slowly.

hypothalamus A part of the brain that lies above the pituitary gland and regulates many body functions.
Through the pituitary gland, the hypothalamus affects the activities of the thyroid, pancreas, parathyroids, adrenals and sex glands. It is involved with the control of body temperature, sexual function, weight, fluid balance and blood pressure.

hypothermia An abnormally low body temperature. Hypothermia is a general cooling of the entire body—the inner core of the body is chilled, so that the body cannot generate heat to stay warm.
For more detailed information, see the ***FIRST AID GUIDE***, *Environmental Emergencies.*

hypothyroidism Condition caused by underactivity of the thyroid gland. Thyroid hormone is involved in a number of processes throughout the body.
Hypothyroidism may be the result of a congenital defect, inflammation of the thyroid gland, or a deficiency of thyroid–stimulating hormone that causes insufficient production of thyroid hormone. Those with hypothyroidism may be overweight, easily tired, intolerant of cold, and suffer dry hair and skin. See ***hyperthyroidism***.

hypoxia A lack of oxygen in the body. A deficiency of oxygen in the body may be caused by a lack of sufficient oxygen in the air breathed, as in mountain climbing or flying at high altitudes, by disease of the lungs that prevents oxygen from reaching the blood, or by a reduction in the blood circulating to the lungs due to heart failure or an obstruction of blood vessels in the lungs.

hysteria An excessive emotional state. A psychiatric

condition in which one responds to anxiety with uncontrolled emotional or physical reaction, as by extreme emotional outbursts, blindness, or loss of speech.

idiosyncrasy Anything unusual in a particular person, such as a mannerism or reaction to a particular food.

ileostomy A surgical procedure in which an opening created in the wall of the abdomen is joined to an opening in the ileum, or lower part of the small intestine, to allow the elimination of body waste.

An ileostomy is created when the colon has been removed because of injury or disease, such as cancer. Waste discharged through the opening is collected in a disposable bag. Once the diet is properly regulated, the ileostomy causes little restriction of normal activities.

immune response The body's natural reaction to any invading organism. Whenever the body is exposed to a foreign element, an ***antibody*** specific to that element, designed to surround and disable it, is fashioned.

In some cases, the immune response proves detrimental, as in the reaction to allergies, transplants, and transfusions. In an allergic reaction, the immune system overreacts to a substance causing unpleasant symptoms, such as itching skin, runny nose, coughing and sneezing, or watery eyes. An allergic reaction may be so mild as to go unnoticed, or it can be so severe as to be life threatening. Of particular concern is the severe reaction called ***anaphylactic shock***, often produced by insect bites, that may cause difficulty in breathing. Each new attack triggers a new response, so that subsequent attacks are usually worse than the previous one.

In the case of a transplant, that is, the deliberate introduction of foreign tissue into the body, there is an attempt to destroy the intruder, making it necessary to introduce drugs to suppress the immune system. Such drugs present the additional hazard of leaving the body open to infection by other organisms that are not beneficial. Transfused blood can also trigger an immune response; it must be of the same type as the recipient's blood so that the immune system will not attempt to destroy it.

immune system See ***allergy*** and ***immunology***

impetigo A highly contagious eruptive infection of the skin, most common in children.

incontinence Inability to control the passage of urine and stool, most often found in infants and the elderly. Incontinence may be an indication of some other condition, such as an obstruction, infection, or illness.

indigestion Impaired digestion; ***dyspepsia***.

infection The presence of an organism, such as a bacterium or virus that can have a harmful effect on the body; indicating any organism that can cause disease; the disease caused by such an organism.

inflammation Redness and swelling, accompanied by heat and pain. Inflammation is the way that living tissue responds to infection—it is symptomatic of the body's protective mechanism at work.

influenza A contagious viral infection of the upper respiratory tract. Influenza is characterized by symptoms similar to a cold, often accompanied by a fever, chills, aching muscles, headache, and a feeling of general malaise.

The flu is unique in its ability to circumvent the immune system, that is, once a population has been infected, the structure of the virus changes so that existing antibodies are not effective in fighting the next attack.

Because influenza spreads so rapidly, it has been surmised that the virus is transmitted by airborne particles from an infected person. Influenza is unpleasant, but seldom serious except for those with a condition that is aggravated by flu symptoms, as a respiratory infection or heart condition. Treatment for the flu is basically the same as for a bad cold; bed rest, extra fluids, and aspirin or aspirin substitute to reduce fever and muscle aches.

An association has been established between administering aspirin for a viral infection and Reye's syndrome in children; therefore, aspirin should not be given to a child with influenza.

ingest To take into the body by eating or absorbing.

inositol See ***vitamin B complex***

insect bites and stings Although an insect bite may be only a minor unpleasantness to most, those who have an allergic reaction may suffer serious consequences. For more information about remedies, see the ***FIRST AID GUIDE****, Medical Emergencies (Insect Bites and Stings).*

In extreme cases, ***anaphylactic shock,*** a severe, potentially fatal, reaction can occur. For more about anaphylactic shock, see the ***FIRST AID GUIDE****, Shock.*

insulin A hormone produced in the pancreas, essential for body cells to absorb sugar. Lack of an adequate insulin supply retards the absorption of sugar, causes it to build up in the bloodstream, and leads to ***diabetes mellitus.*** An excess of insulin can cause overabsorption by the cells and create a low level of sugar in the blood called ***hypoglycemia*** that can lead to ***insulin shock***.

insulin shock An abnormal condition that occurs when there is an excess amount of insulin in the body in relation to the amount of sugar available that causes overabsorption by the cells and a corresponding reduction of the level of sugar in the blood.

For more information about symptoms and treatment, see the ***FIRST AID GUIDE****, Medical Emergencies.*

internist A physician who specializes in the diagnosis and non–surgical treatment of disease.

intestines Lower part of the alimentary canal, extending from stomach to anus; the large and small intestines.

ischemia A deficiency of blood in an organ or part of the body. Ischemia is caused by obstruction of the blood vessels that supply an organ or area of the body. Such obstruction may be the result of narrowing, compression, or damage from conditions such as a blood clot or ***atherosclerosis*** and causes oxygen loss that leads to tissue death in the affected area.

jaundice A condition caused by bile pigments in the blood, characterized by a yellowing of the skin and other tissue.

joint The juncture of two or more bones.

For a more detailed description, see the ***FIRST AID GUIDE****, A Short Course in Anatomy.*

kidney One of a pair of abdominal organs that removes water and waste matter from the blood and excretes them as urine.

kidney failure The condition that exists when the kidneys cease normal function, causing the buildup of toxic substances within the body. Kidney failure may be caused by any of several conditions, such as blockage of the urinary tract as by kidney stones, an adverse reaction to medication, an infectious disease that attacks the kidney, heart attack, severe dehydration, serious injury, or a congenital condition, one that exists from birth.

Kidney failure may be acute, a sudden malfunction that causes a buildup of toxins within the body in a matter of hours; or it may be chronic, a malfunction of the kidneys that grows progressively worse, with a gradual buildup of toxins that may occur over a span of months or years.

The most common symptom of kidney failure is a reduction in the output of urine that causes an accumulation of fluid in tissues. As the body becomes more toxic, the subject experiences constant fatigue, loss of appetite, diarrhea, nausea and difficulty in breathing. If the condition remains untreated, coma and death will follow.

kidney stone A mineral formation lodged in the urinary tract; a *calculus*. Kidney stones are formed when excess minerals such as calcium are present and concentrate into a hard lump. Excess calcium in the system may come from foods with a high calcium content or those rich in vitamin D that aids in absorption of calcium, or from calcium released by fractured bones. Other factors may also contribute to formation of stones: uric acid may crystallize into stones; urine retained as the result of infection can contain elements that solidify.

When a stone becomes large enough, or becomes positioned so that it causes notice, it may produce considerable pain in the area, frequent and painful urination, blood in the urine, nausea, or chills and fever. A stone that becomes lodged in the ureter, the channel from the kidney to the bladder, can produce severe pain in the back, abdomen and groin. In any incidence of these symptoms, immediate medical attention is required.

Kidney stones that are too small to be noticed may still cause damage to delicate tissues in the urinary tract.

laceration A jagged cut or wound.

laryngitis Inflammation of the larynx.

The larynx is the voice box located in the upper part of the respiratory tract. Infection is manifested by a hoarse or grating voice, or occasionally, a complete loss of speech. Laryngitis may be caused by an infection, such as that accompanying a cold or flu, from irritation of the mucous membrane of the larynx, as by smoking, dust, or air pollution, or from straining the voice. In addition to altered speech, the sufferer may also experience a scratchy feeling in the throat and pain when speaking.

The best treatment for laryngitis is a total resting of the

vocal cords and, if necessary, throat spray, aspirin, or acetaminophen to relieve discomfort. Persistent or frequent recurrence may be symptomatic of a more serious condition, and should be referred to a physician.

Legionnaires' disease A severe bacterial infection of the respiratory tract. The disease gets its name from its first noted outbreak—in 1976, among those attending a convention of the American Legion in Philadelphia. Subsequently, earlier outbreaks of the disease were identified.

Onset of the disease may be mild, emulating the onset of influenza. Later symptoms are similar to those of any respiratory infection: coughing, shortness of breath, chest and abdominal pain, headache, fever, nausea, vomiting, and diarrhea. Although outbreaks of the disease are infrequent, because of its life–threatening nature, it should be suspected in any respiratory infection that gets progressively worse over a period of several days, especially among the elderly or chronically ill.

leprosy A mildly contagious, chronic bacterial infection that causes loss of sensation.

lesion An alteration in the condition of tissue, that may be caused by injury, disease, abnormal growth, etc.

lethargy An unnatural lack of energy; sluggishness.

leukemia Any of a number of deadly diseases of the white blood cells and bone marrow.

Leukemia originates in bone marrow, causing excessive production of white blood cells, many of which are immature or damaged. These ineffective white blood cells reduce the body's ability to fight infection while crowding out the red blood cells that carry oxygen throughout the body, and platelets that are necessary for clotting.

leukocyte Any of the colorless cells found in the blood, lymph, or tissues, vital to the body's defense against disease or infection; a white blood cell.

ligament Tough fibrous tissue that holds bones together at a joint and supports body organs.

lipoma A benign tumor of fatty tissue.

liver The largest gland in the body, located in the upper part of the abdominal cavity.

The liver performs a number of functions, including the manufacture of substances necessary for blood clotting, the processing of nutrients absorbed by the small intestine, and the removal of toxic substances from the blood.

lockjaw See ***tetanus***

lumbago Rheumatic pain in the lower back; often used to describe any back pain.

lymphocyte A type of white blood cell that develops in lymphatic tissue. Lymphocytes are extremely important to the body's immune system—they direct immune responses, identify the characteristics of ***antigens***, and produce the antibodies to combine with and destroy them.

malady Any condition that exhibits symptoms of illness or disease.

malaise A general feeling of discomfort or physical decline that may indicate the onset of disease.

malignant Descriptive of that which is a danger to health and well–being; likely to cause death.

mastoid bone The bone directly behind the ear.

mastoiditis A bacterial infection of the air cells in the mastoid bone. Mastoiditis is usually caused by the spread of infection from the middle ear. In severe cases, the infection is in danger of reaching the interior of the skull.

measles A contagious viral disease common among children; *rubeola*. The virus may be spread by moisture from the nose of throat of an infected person who is usually contagious for several days before symptoms are apparent and up to six days after the rash appears.

Early symptoms are similar to those of a cold—runny

nose, congestion, sneezing, watery eyes, coughing and fever. After several days there is a sensitivity to bright light, the fever drops, and characteristic spots may appear in the mouth. Soon after, the fever rises and a rash appears, usually about the face, neck, and behind the ears before spreading over the entire body. The rash first appears as red spots; as they multiply, they grow together to form irregular blotches. Usually within days, the fever subsides and the condition improves.

Although the disease is relatively mild, anyone contracting measles should be placed under a doctor's care in order to avoid complications such as ***pneumonia***, ***encephalitis***, ear infection, ***bronchitis***, etc.

As with all viral infections, aspirin should not be administered to children because of the harmful link that has been established with Reye's syndrome.

melanoma A tumor of cells containing dark pigment, usually malignant.

Meniere's disease

A disorder of the inner ear caused by a buildup of fluid. The canals, or labyrinth, of the inner ear serve to control balance and equilibrium by noting movements of the head and sending the information to the brain. Any disruption of this function can cause dizziness, nausea, vomiting, and distorted perception of surroundings, as when furniture appears to be spinning around a room.

Meniere's disease results from an increase in pressure from a buildup of fluid that distorts and, sometimes, ruptures the lining of the walls in the inner ear. A mild attack may last less than an hour or several days, then disappear. Attacks may recur at intervals of weeks or months. Severe attacks, that make normal movement impossible require confinement to bed. In such attacks, bizarre illusions may accompany any head movement, the subject may suffer migraine headaches and some loss of hearing.

middle ear infection The middle ear transfers sound vibrations to the inner ear and protects the eardrum from rupture by equalizing inside pressure with that outside the body. Such equalization is made possible by the *eustachian tube* that connects the middle ear with the throat. The eustachian tube is also the culprit that makes the middle ear susceptible to infection—most ailments of the middle ear are caused by virus or bacteria in the nose or throat that travel to the ear through the eustachian tube.

A middle ear infection can cause severe throbbing pain, hearing loss, fever, dizziness, nausea, or vomiting. In extreme cases, pressure against the eardrum may cause it to burst, creating a danger of spreading the infection.

Because of the danger of hearing loss and spreading infection, a physician should be consulted in any case of ear infection.

mononucleosis A contagious viral disease that attacks the lymph nodes; *infectious mononucleosis*.

Mononucleosis is characterized by sore throat, fever, swollen glands, and a feeling of weakness. Onset of the infection is so subtle that it appears to be no more than a simple cold; however, a sore throat that persists for more than a week with swollen glands in the throat and neck accompanied by fever and weakness may be a sign of mononucleosis. The usual treatment is rest and lots of liquids until temperature returns to normal.

Generally, mononucleosis is uncomplicated, although occasionally the infection spreads to the liver or spleen, signaled by ***jaundice*** and pain or tenderness in the abdomen. Either condition should be referred to a physician.

multiple sclerosis A chronic disease of the nervous system. The condition is the result of random destruction of the *myelin sheaths* that insulate nerve cells.

Multiple sclerosis usually affects young adults, causing weakness or paralysis in parts of the body, blurred vision, muscle spasms or incontinence. It then commonly goes into remission that may last several years, but recurring attacks can cause increasing disability.

mumps A contagious viral disease common among children. Mumps may begin with fever, headache, sore throat, or earache followed by painful swelling of the salivary glands that may cause difficulty in eating. Other glands and organs may become infected and swollen as well, such as the testes, ovaries, pancreas, liver, etc.

muscle Tissue made up of fibers that have the ability to contract. It is through the contraction of muscle that all movements of the body are enabled.

Voluntary muscles, also known as striated muscles are, with one notable exception, consciously controlled by the individual. Involuntary muscles, also known as smooth muscles, such as those found in the blood vessels, digestive system, respiratory system, etc., are not under conscious control. The exception to this ordering is a group of striated heart muscles that are controlled by the motor nerves rather than the conscious will.

myasthenia gravis A ***neuromuscular*** disorder characterized by a slow and progressive paralysis.

Myasthenia gravis is caused by failure of the muscles to receive messages transmitted by nerves causing paralysis, although the muscles do not atrophy, or waste away.

Signs of the disease usually show up first in the face as paralysis of the eye muscles that causes squinting or double vision, sagging of the cheeks, and difficulty in talking, chewing, or swallowing. The arms and legs may be affected, causing difficulty in walking or in the accomplishment of everyday tasks, like lifting a fork. Eventually, breathing may be impaired. The severity of symptoms varies from day to day and even throughout the day, with a tendency to be more oppressive at night.

There is usually no cure for myasthenia gravis, although there are drugs that can restore nerve transmission and improve muscle strength.

narcolepsy A disorder characterized by sudden, uncontrolled lapses into deep, but brief, sleep. Attacks may be related to another condition, although they often occur with no other symptoms: the subject simply falls into a deep sleep and awakens refreshed.

nausea A feeling that one wants to vomit, brought on by anything that interferes with the flow through the digestive tract, whether direct, as by tainted food or infection, or indirect, as by emotional or psychological response.

Nausea may be manifested as discomfort or a burning sensation in the abdomen or chest, excessive secretion of saliva, sweating, blurred vision or feelings of weakness.

necrosis Death of tissue in the midst of healthy tissue.

Necrosis takes place when cells are destroyed by infection or when they are cut off from their blood supply. It may occur in an area of the body served by vessels that have been injured or blocked, in areas of the heart following a heart attack, or in the midst of a tumor that has outgrown its blood supply.

neoplasm An abnormal growth of cells or tissue; a tumor.

nephrology The branch of medicine that deals with the diagnosis and treatment of kidney disorders.

nervous system The network of cells that receive and transmit signals to coordinate the various parts of the body and the organs controlling body functions.

For more detailed information, see the ***FIRST AID GUIDE***, *Shock*.

neuralgia Any pain along the course of a nerve.

The cause of neuralgia is not always apparent, although

there may be evidence of inflammation or damage. The condition may be slight and fleeting, or may involve a severe pain or one that is longer lasting.

Shingles, or *herpes zoster* is characterized by intense pain and infection along the course of a nerve. ***Sciatica,*** caused by pressure on the sciatic nerve, is experienced as an ache or a recurring tingling sensation in the buttock and along the back of the thigh. ***Carpal tunnel syndrome*** causes tingling in the fingers that may progress to pain running up the arm as a result of pressure on the large nerve that passes through the wrist. Treatment for these and other conditions that cause neuralgia varies with the cause, location and severity of the condition.

neuritis Any inflammation of a nerve. Neuritis may be brought on by infection, by pressure on the nerve, by exposure to toxins, by loss of the nerve's blood supply, or by lack of a vital substances in the diet. Neuritis can cause discomfort that ranges from tingling to severe pain, a loss of sensation and muscle control, or even paralysis. Treatment varies depending on the cause.

neurology The branch of medicine concerned with the diagnosis and treatment of disorders that have an effect on the nervous system. The nervous system comprises the brain, the spinal cord and the network of peripheral nerves that flow throughout the body.

neuromuscular Affecting both nerve and muscle.

neurosis An emotional or psychological disorder. Usually manifested by anxiety or depression; commonly caused by inability to adjust to the ordinary stresses of life.

neurotransmitter A substance that transmits nerve impulses between nerve cells. The basic unit of the nervous system is the nerve cell, or neuron. At the ends of each nerve cell are numerous sacs containing neurotransmitter chemicals that are released by nerve impulses traveling through the nerve cell. Upon release, the neurotransmitters jump to the next nerve cell to stimulate the production of an impulse to carry the signal on.

nosebleed Bleeding from the nose caused by a rupture in the vessels in the inner lining of the nose.

For more information about causes and treatment, see the ***FIRST AID GUIDE***, *Controlling Bleeding.*

Nosebleeds that are difficult to stop or recur regularly should be referred to a physician.

nutriment A source of nutrition. Material taken in to sustain life and promote growth.

obesity The condition of being considerably overweight.

obsession That which engages a person's consciousness to an abnormal degree. Obsession may take the form of irrational concerns, repetitive actions, doubts, or fears that cannot be avoided or dismissed. Obsessions may be linked, as for one who repeatedly checks door locks because of obsession with security. An obsession may be a symptom of a psychiatric illness or of a brain disorder.

obstetrics/gynecology *Obstetrics* is the branch of medicine dealing with conditions related to pregnancy and childbirth. *Gynecology* is concerned with diagnosis and treatment of disorders of the female reproductive system. Because of the close relationship between the two fields, they are often practiced as a single specialty.

occult blood Blood in such small quantities that it cannot be easily detected. Usually describes blood passed off in the feces that can only be detected under a microscope; often a sign of bleeding in the gastrointestinal tract.

ocularist One who fashions and fits artificial eyes.

oliguria An abnormal reduction in the passage of urine. Oliguria may be a sign of kidney failure or other disease.

oncology The study of the cause and treatment of abnormal tissue growth. Oncology deals with tumors, particularly those that are malignant, or cancerous. Because of the close association with cancers of the blood, many oncologists are also hematologists, qualified to deal with diseases of the blood.

ophthalmology The branch of medical science dealing with the study of the eye as well as diagnoses, and treatment of diseases and injuries to the eye. The ophthalmologist, who is a physician, may also qualify as a surgeon who can reattach retinas, remove cataracts, etc. There are also non–medical fields that deal with the eyes, such as the *optometrist*, who tests the eyes, the *optician*, who fashions lenses and fits corrective lenses according to prescription from an ophthalmologist or optometrist, and the *ocularist*, who fashions and fits artificial eyes.

ophthalmoplegia Weakness or paralysis of the muscles of the eye. Ophthalmoplegia affects the muscles that control eye movements as well as dilation and contraction of the pupil. It can be caused by any condition that impacts on the muscles or the nerves that control them, as a head injury, stroke, tumor, etc.

opium An addictive narcotic, obtained from the juice of the opium poppy; the source of morphine, heroin, codeine and other medicinal compounds. It engenders a feeling of euphoria, relieves pain and hunger, and, in time, brings on drowsiness and sleep. Most users become physically and emotionally dependent on the drug.

optician One who fashions lenses and fits glasses or contact lenses.

optometrist One who tests the eyes for fitting out with corrective lenses.

orthodontia The branch of dentistry that deals with the correcting of irregularities of the teeth.

orthopedics The branch of medicine that deals with disease and injury of the muscles, bones, and joints.

ossification The transformation of soft tissue into bone or bone–like tissue.

osteoarthritis A degenerative disease of the joints. Osteoarthritis is generally associated with age, and is most prevalent in joints weakened by a prior injury or disease, or those subjected to unusual stress, as lower body weight–bearing joints, especially among the overweight.

The condition is caused by loss of cartilage that normally protects the ends of the bones: as space between bones narrows, they grate to cause wear or displacement and ultimately, inflammation, swelling, pain, and stiffness.

osteoma A benign tumor comprised of bone. An osteoma is seldom troublesome unless it is positioned to cause pressure on a nerve. The growth may appear anywhere in the body, but is most often attached to a normal bone, especially of the skull and the lower jaw.

osteomalacia Softening of bone caused by a lack of vitamin D that is necessary for the absorption and utilization of calcium in the body. Vitamin D is formed in the skin from exposure to sunlight and is available in the diet in dairy products and in fish oils.

In some areas, a lack of winter sunlight contributes to the deficiency; however, regular doses of cod liver oil can overcome the problem. A deficiency may also be caused by a condition that inhibits absorption, or by an increased requirement for the vitamin, as in pregnancy. Osteomalacia causes pain and tenderness in the bones, and may lead to bone fractures and weakness of the muscles.

osteoporosis A condition marked by a decrease in calcium content in the bones. As the body ages, the bones thin to some extent; when there is a lack of calcium available to the body, the process is hastened and the bones become especially susceptible to fracture.

The onset of osteoporosis may escape notice, or it may

cause pain in the lower back, often following the fracture of a vertebra. Such fractures tend to be patterned, so that over a period of time, subsequent fracturing of vertebrae may lead to deformity of the spine and difficulty walking that can make one susceptible to further injury.

Osteoporosis is a leading factor in hip injuries among the elderly. The best defense is a carefully monitored light exercise that strengthens the muscles supporting bones that have become weakened. Diet is also any important factor, especially one that provides adequate vitamin D and calcium to promote the formation of bone.

osteosarcoma A malignant tumor of the bone. Osteosarcoma usually occurs in the long bones of the arm or leg. Most common in children and young adults, it typically spreads to the lungs which is usually fatal.

otorhinolaryngology The medical specialty that combines the study, diagnosis and treatment for diseases of the ears, nose and throat. Because of the linkage of the passages—ears and throat are linked by the eustachian tubes; nose and throat meet at the nasopharynx—infections in one organ are commonly spread to another.

otosclerosis A growth of spongy bone in the ear that causes progressive deafness. In otosclerosis, the stapes, one of the bones in the middle ear that transmits sound waves to the inner ear, is overgrown and immobilized, so that the transmission of sound vibrations is impaired. The condition may be corrected by a surgical procedure in which the stapes is replaced—a very delicate procedure that carries some risk of failure.

oxygen A colorless, odorless gas that occurs free in the atmosphere. Oxygen, essential to the body, is absorbed from the lungs into the bloodstream, where it is carried by the hemoglobin in the red blood cells to be discharged to the tissues. The brain is most sensitive to oxygen deprivation and is permanently damaged if its supply is cut off for more than a few minutes.

pacemaker A network of muscle fibers in the right ventricle of the heart that control the rhythm of heartbeat; an artificial device that stimulates and regularizes the heartbeat by periodic discharge of electrical impulses.

It is the function of the natural pacemaker in the heart to cause it to beat at a regular tempo that allows the proper flow of blood through it. When that natural function is impaired by injury or disease, an artificial pacemaker may be implanted in the heart to take over the function.

pain Severe discomfort that may be physical, as caused by disease or injury, or emotional, as caused by grief or depression. The mechanics of pain are not thoroughly understood, but pain assists greatly in diagnosis of disease or injury as by location, type, or duration of discomfort.

palate The roof of the mouth, that consists of a firm *hard palate* in the front and a fleshy *soft palate* in the back, toward the throat.

palliative Descriptive of medication that alleviates pain or other symptoms, but does not have the power to heal.

palpitation Rapid beating, especially of the heart.

palsy Any of a number of diseases characterized by tremors, weakness of the muscles, or an odd gait and attitude; ***paralysis***.

pancreas A large gland located near the stomach at the back of the abdominal cavity that secretes enzymes to aid in digestion and hormones to regulate blood sugar.

The enzymes are released to the small intestine to help break down carbohydrates, proteins, and fats.

Hormones produced include insulin, that aids in the utilization of glucose, or blood sugar, and glucagon, that prompts the liver to release stored sugar into the blood.

paralysis Impairment or loss of muscle function. Paralysis may be caused by disease or injury to the muscle or nerves that direct it and may range from impairing a single muscle or nerve to affecting a large part of the body. Disease of the muscle itself commonly leads to weakness rather than paralysis, although certain forms of *muscular dystrophy* can cause severe and ultimately fatal paralysis. Any blockage of impulse from nerves to muscles caused by direct injury or by disease may cause either weakness or lead to total paralysis, depending on the condition. Recovery, too, depends on the underlying cause, as in some situations there is total remission while in others there is virtually no hope for recovery.

paranoia A mental disorder typified by delusions of persecution and grandeur. Paranoia is characterized by suspicion that innocent acts are direct personal attacks, coupled with an exaggerated feeling of self worth that the subject feels is unrecognized or unjustly ignored.

paraplegia Paralysis of the lower part of the body. Paraplegia, usually caused by damage to the spinal cord, may affect only the use of the lower limbs, or it may encompass the lower trunk as well causing dysfunction of the bladder and rectum.

parasite Anything that lives in or on another from which it gains sustenance or protection without returning any benefit, and perhaps doing harm to its host.

Parkinson's disease A nervous disorder characterized primarily by tremor, muscle rigidity and a jerky gait. The condition may be marked by uncontrollable shaking, difficulty in starting to move, a stooped posture, and expressionless face. Shaking may be more noticeable with tension or excitement, or when resting. In the later stages, speech, eating, and writing become more difficult. Parkinson's disease is progressive; it may be present in a mild form for years with little change, or it can lead to severe disability within a few years.

pasteurization The process of heating a liquid to maintain a temperature of 60 to 70C. for about forty minutes. Pasteurization destroys organisms that cause fermentation, thus retarding spoilage as well as exterminating those that cause disease.

patch test A test to determine sensitivity to specific irritants. Allergy, or excessive sensitivity to substances such as pollen, feathers, or dust is the cause of hay fever and hives, and may be the cause of asthma, eczema, and sinusitis. When the cause is not apparent, a patch test may determine the irritants that cause the reaction.

The patch test is administered by applying a small spot of an irritant to the skin and checking for a reaction in one to two days. Because of the large number of possibilities, several irritants are usually tested at one time. Testing continues with different sets until it is determined which irritants cause a reaction, and treatment can begin.

pathology The branch of medical science concerned with determination of the causes, symptoms and effects of disease as well as the means by which the spread of a disease may be limited.

There are a number of specialties within the field of pathology. Best known, perhaps, is *forensic pathology,* charged with the gathering of information, as from an autopsy, to be used as evidence in a court of law.

pediatrics The branch of medical science that deals with the diseases and care of children.

pellagra A disease caused by a deficiency of niacin a part of the complex of B vitamins, present in meat, eggs, vegetables and fruit. Signs of pellagra are reddening of exposed skin, loss of appetite, and irritability. The condition is common among alcoholics.

pelvis The pelvis is a basin–shaped bony structure at the lower portion of the ***trunk*** below the movable ***vertebrae*** of the ***spinal column***, which it supports, and above the lower limbs, upon which it rests. Four bones compose the pelvis: the two bones of the backbone and the wing–shaped hip bones on either side. The pelvis forms the floor of the ***abdominal cavity*** and provides deep sockets in which the heads of the thigh bones fit.

peptic ulcer Any erosion, or open sore, in the area of the digestive tract exposed to pepsin, an enzyme formed in the stomach that aids in digestion of protein. It is believed that peptic ulcers result from excessive excretions of pepsin irritating the lower end of the esophagus, the stomach, or the duodenum, the first portion of the small intestine. Natural weakness in the wall of the stomach may also contribute, as does stress and heredity.

The onset of ulcers may be subtle, exhibiting symptoms that can be taken for indigestion; however, when the symptoms occur after every meal, during stress, and occasionally before meals, a physician should be consulted.

pericarditis Inflammation of the pericardium, the membrane that surrounds the heart. It may be associated with other ailments, such as pneumonia or heart attack, or caused by bacteria from an open wound.

The condition is marked by chest pains that intensify with breathing, coughing, or lying down. Other illnesses with similar symptoms are equally serious; therefore, any incident of chest pain should be referred to a physician.

Constrictive pericarditis occurs when inflammation causes thickening of the pericardium that restricts heart action. The condition is marked by difficulty breathing, swollen neck veins and accumulation of fluid in the legs.

periodontics The branch of dentistry that deals with the treatment of diseases and disorders of the *periodontium*, that is, the gum and tissues surrounding and supporting the teeth.

peritonitis Inflammation of the *peritoneum*, the membrane that lines the abdominal cavity, caused when one of the hollow organs of the abdomen is perforated, when infection is spread from an inflamed organ, or when the abdominal cavity is breached by a wound.

The condition is marked by intense pain, and a tender and rigid abdominal wall. There may be nausea, vomiting, and dehydration. Peritonitis is extremely serious and requires immediate medical attention.

pertussis See ***whooping cough***

phantom limb syndrome The illusion by an amputee that a missing limb is still in place. The individual may experience feelings of touch, heat, cold, pain, etc. Usually sensations disappear as the subject recuperates, but they may last for a time or reappear without notice.

pharmaceutics, pharmacy The precise preparation and dispensing of medicines according to the instructions of a physician. The pharmacist also has the knowledge to advise on the use of non–prescription medications.

pharmacology The study and acquired knowledge of the nature and action of drugs.

pharyngitis Inflammation of the *pharynx*, the passage that connects the back of the mouth and nose with the larynx and the esophagus; a sore throat.

phlebitis Painful inflammation of a vein evidenced by swelling and sensitivity in the area of the inflammation.

pituitary gland A tiny organ located just beneath the base of the brain that produces a number of hormones that direct the functions of other glands and organs throughout the body.

platelet A disk–shaped structure in the blood that plays a critical part in clotting; *thrombocytes*.

Normally, blood flows without change in its chemistry;

however, when a blood vessel is ruptured and the blood comes into contact with foreign tissue, clotting begins. *Platelets* in the blood, triggered by the contact, release a chemical that begins a chain reaction involving a number of protein constituents in the blood, ending with the conversion of fibrinogen, a soluble material, to fibrin, that is insoluble. The fibrin is laid down in fine strands that collect white and red blood cells to form a clot.

pleurisy Inflammation of the pleura, membranes that cover the outer surface of the lungs. Lubricated by pleural fluid, they serve to reduce friction of chest members as the lungs expand and contract. Pleurisy frequently occurs as a complication of a respiratory tract infection, such as pneumonia, though there are other causes.

Dry pleurisy describes the condition where the infected pleurae rub against each other; *wet pleurisy* is characterized by a condition in which fluid from the infected tissue fills the space between the lungs and the wall of the chest cavity. In either case, breathing is painful and difficult. Breathing capacity may be especially reduced in the case of wet pleurisy because the fluid in the chest cavity tends to compress the lungs.

In addition to severe chest pains that force shallow breathing, there is usually fever and a painful cough.

pneumonia Inflammation of the lungs, in which the air sacs, the alveoli, fill with fluid and white blood cells.

Pneumonia is classified primarily according to the location of the inflammation: *lobar pneumonia* is usually confined to one section, or lobe, of the lung; *double pneumonia* affects both lungs; *bronchial pneumonia* is concentrated in and about the bronchi, the airways that connect the windpipe and the air cells of the lungs; *walking pneumonia* is a relatively mild condition that may not be readily identified as a lung infection.

Pneumonia may be caused by bacteria, virus, fungi or other microorganisms. Any foreign matter, as a chemical, that is inhaled may carry an agent that causes infection. Any drug or disease that inhibits the immune system may make one increasingly susceptible to an attack. Pneumonia commonly occurs when resistance is lowered. It may be brought on when the body's defenses are strained from fighting the ravages of a cold, influenza, emphysema, asthma, etc. Any condition that requires confinement to bed for a long period increases susceptibility to pneumonia, especially in the elderly.

Pneumonia is usually characterized by chest pain, fever, coughing, and difficulty in breathing. Pneumonia caused by a viral infection may be accompanied by the symptoms normally associated the a cold or flu. Other forms of pneumonia may strike suddenly with chills, shivering, an abrupt rise in temperature, shallow breathing, and the discharge of dark yellow or bloody sputum.

Treatment for pneumonia should be prescribed by a physician, and usually involves bed rest, plenty of fluids and a soft diet. If the condition is secondary to another, treatment of the primary condition is important in order to strengthen the body's immune system. Bacterial pneumonia may be treated with antibiotics.

In very serious cases, or where there is continued labored breathing, hospital care may be necessary.

podiatry The science that deals with diseases, irregularities and injuries of the foot; chiropody.

Not all problems of the feet require a specialist, but some, such as correction of a deformity occurring at birth, should be in the hands of one likely to be most knowledgeable about the latest techniques. The podiatrist often fills a special need by performing normal foot care that the elderly or incapacitated cannot perform for themselves, and by the knowledge and treatment of those conditions that most effect the elderly.

poisoning Introduction into the body of any substance in a quantity that is harmful or destructive. Poisoning may be caused by a non–toxic or even beneficial substance, as a medication in combination with another substance, or in a large quantity that makes it harmful. It may be in the form an air pollutant or bacterial growth in tainted food. Poisoning can produce unpleasant symptoms, such as abdominal cramps, nausea, vomiting, sweating, or weakness. It can also cause delirium, loss of consciousness, difficulty breathing, blindness, paralysis and death. Certain poisons may be neutralized or passed off while others accumulate in the system until they become damaging. Some cases of poisoning have no lasting effect while others cause scarring or other conditions that remain and may get worse in time. Treatment for poisoning may be as simple as cleansing the offending substance from the body or administering an antidote, or it may require extended treatment to correct the resulting damage.

poliomyelitis Inflammation of the spinal cord that can cause paralysis; *infantile paralysis*; *polio*. Poliomyelitis is a viral infection, spread by inhalation or ingestion of dust or fecal matter, that can reach epidemic proportions. Infection initially causes discomfort or cramps in the muscles, sore throat, and a stiffness in the neck and spine. Symptoms may recede within a few days or they may spread throughout the system, causing paralysis, atrophy of the muscles and, in some cases, permanent disability. Immunization is so widespread that poliomyelitis has been practically eradicated in the United States.

pollutant Something that contaminates, or makes impure.

polyp A projecting growth of mucous membrane, usually not malignant.

proctology The branch of medical science that deals with diseases and disorders of the anus and rectum.

prognosis A prediction of the probable course of a disease or disability and the forecast for recovery.

prosthesis An artificial device that replaces a natural part of the body. The most common prosthetic device replaces missing teeth: dentures, false teeth, partial plates, etc. Others include artificial limbs; replacement joints, as for the hip, knee, elbow, etc.; replacement valves for the heart; and replacement lenses for the eye. Some devices are strictly cosmetic, such as an artificial eye that has no function except to replace one lost to disease or injury.

proteinuria Presence of protein in urine. ***Albuminuria*** is virtually the same as proteinuria, as albumin is the only protein detected in significant amounts in the urine.

psoriasis A chronic skin disease characterized by reddish patches with silvery scales. Psoriasis is not contagious.

psychiatry The branch of medicine dealing with diagnosis and treatment of mental and emotional diseases and disorders. In addition to the treatment of *psychoses*, or severe mental disorders, psychiatry is involved in the treatment and rehabilitation of those suffering from behavioral disorders, anxiety, depression, addiction, etc. The *psychiatrist* is a medical doctor with training in psychology and is therefore authorized to prescribe medication as a part of therapy; the *psychologist*, on the other hand, does not have a medical degree and thus cannot prescribe drugs.

psychology The science that deals with human behavior; the study of mental and emotional processes.

psychosis A severe personality disorder in which contact with reality is seriously impaired. Psychosis may be the result of malfunction of the mind without apparent organic cause, or it may be caused by injury or disease.

psychosomatic Descriptive of a physical ailment that originates in a mental or emotional disorder.

pulmonary medicine The branch of medicine that deals with the study, diagnosis, and treatment of diseases and disorders of the lungs, such as cancer, tuberculosis, pneumonia, bronchitis, pleurisy, and emphysema.

purpura The presence of blood in the skin or mucous membranes. Purpura is caused by defects in the walls of capillaries that have not been sealed off by platelets. The condition is evidenced by tiny red or purple spots appearing on the surface of the skin or mucous membrane.

pus A yellowish–white fluid in which dead leukocytes, dead tissue, etc. are suspended; the result of an infection.

quarantine Isolation of those exposed to a communicable disease. The purpose of a quarantine is to avoid contact with others so as to prevent spread of the disease, especially when there is danger of an epidemic, or rapid spread throughout the community.

Quarantine is not necessarily limited to those who show signs of being infected. After exposure to certain diseases, one who is susceptible may be infected and not show symptoms, although the disease can be passed on. By isolating the person or persons for the longest known incubation time of the disease, there is reasonable assurance that the infection will not be spread.

rabies An infectious, fatal, viral disease of animals that can be transmitted to man. The rabies virus is contained in the animal's saliva; humans usually contract the disease from the bite of an infected animal.

Early symptoms are depression, restlessness and fever followed by a period of hyperactivity, abnormal salivation, and painful spasms of the muscles in the throat. Usually, the victim develops an aversion to water, being unable to drink despite an irrepressible thirst. An untreated case is usually fatal in three to ten days.

Treatment of any possible exposure should be prompt. After a bite or exposure of an open wound to animal saliva, the area should be completely washed with soap and water and swabbed with an antiseptic; then medical help should be sought. A domestic animal that does not exhibit symptoms should be confined and observed. A wild animal or any animal that shows symptoms of being rabid should be captured by an experienced professional.

radiation therapy The treatment of disease by the use of radioactive materials. Such treatment may be by material contained in a device that can be inserted directly into the tissues or a body cavity, by injection, or in a drink.

radiology The branch of medicine that treats of the use of radioactive substances in diagnosis and treatment. *Diagnostic radiology* is mainly involved with reproducing an image of part of the body on X–ray film. To improve the image quality and subsequent analysis, special dyes called *contrast media* may be used. Radiologists also use sound waves or magnetic impulses to create images. *Radiation oncology* is a special field concerned with radiation as a treatment for cancer.

rash A skin eruption, usually red spots or patches, often with minor irritation, as itching. A rash may be symptomatic of a number of conditions, including blocked sweat glands, allergy, viral or bacterial infection, etc.

reflex An automatic, involuntary, or learned response to a stimulus. Most of the actions of the body that allow it to function normally are reflex actions, such as the release of perspiration to adjust body heat, the secretion of digestive juices when food is ingested, or the adjustment of the eye to accommodate available light.

Many such reflexes are controllable; for example, closing the eye when an object is brought near may be overcome to allow examination. Many reflexes are learned as well: experience often dictates whether one ducks or tries to catch a thrown object. The failure of the body to respond in a normal or expected way to stimuli may be a sign of disruption in the neural function.

respiration Inhaling and exhaling; the exchange of oxygen and carbon dioxide between outside air and lungs.

respiratory arrest A cessation of breathing.

Breathing may stop as a result of a variety of serious accidents. The most common causes are overdose of narcotics; electric shock which can cause paralysis of the nerve centers that control breathing and stop or alter regular beat of the heart; suffocation; drowning which is a form of suffocation in which air to the lungs is cut off by water or spasms of the larynx; poisonous gas such as carbon monoxide, sulfur dioxide, oxides of nitrogen, ammonia, or hydrogen cyanide; head injuries; and heart problems.

For more information about symptoms and treatment, see the ***FIRST AID GUIDE****, Artificial Ventilation.*

respiratory system The system by which oxygen is taken into the body and carbon dioxide discharged; the nose, throat, larynx, trachea, bronchi and lungs.

For a more detailed description, see the ***FIRST AID GUIDE****, A Short Course in Anatomy.*

retina The light–sensitive organ at the back of the eye that receives images from the lens that are transmitted through the optic nerve to the brain.

Reye's syndrome A serious disease in which inflammation of the brain is coupled with liver damage.

Reye's syndrome is a rare condition that usually infects children recovering from a viral infection, such as chicken pox. A relationship has been established between the disease and the administering of aspirin for a viral infection; no exact cause for the disease is known.

Onset of infection is characterized by sudden vomiting, hyperactivity or sleepiness, and confusion. Convulsions and coma may follow. Immediate diagnosis is essential as the first few days are usually the most critical.

rheumatic fever An infectious disease characterized by swelling of the joints and inflammation of heart valves. Rheumatic fever, most common in children, is brought about by an allergic reaction following a bacterial infection of the throat.

The condition causes painful inflammation and swelling as joints of the ankles, knees, and wrists are infected; large, irregular skin rashes; and fever. Inflammation of heart valves may cause permanent damage due to formation of scar tissue. Problems may surface years after when the overworked heart becomes enlarged.

Any time throat infection is followed within a few weeks by fever and inflammation of joints, rheumatic fever should be considered, and a physician consulted.

rheumatic heart disease A complication of an attack of ***rheumatic fever***. Rheumatic fever, as noted above, may cause inflammation of the heart valves that results in the formation of scar tissue. The valves thus damaged may function without symptoms of impairment for years.

Although it is possible for the heart to compensate for the damage so that there is no serious disability, significant problems may occur. The scarring can cause a narrowing of the valve that restricts the flow of blood. Blood clots may form to further restrict the flow of blood out of the heart and lead to a number of symptoms associated with the deprivation of oxygen in the organs of the body.

Under the care of a physician, a program of regular exercise and proper diet can, in most cases, minimize the effects of rheumatic heart disease.

rheumatology The branch of medicine that deals with

the study, diagnosis, and treatment of rheumatic diseases, that is, those concerned with connective tissue, such as bones and muscles.

Rh factor An ***antigen*** that is present in some blood. The Rh, or rhesus, factor, named for the monkey in which it was first discovered, is found in blood, designated *Rh–positive*. *Rh–negative* blood is lacking the Rh factor.

If Rh–positive blood is introduced into the bloodstream of one who has Rh–negative blood, an ***antibody*** is produced when the immune system views it as an invader.

Mixing of the bloods can come about in two ways: by transfusion or through the mixing of the blood of an Rh–negative mother with that of a child who has inherited Rh–positive blood from the father. In either case, Rh–negative system will form antibodies to trap and destroy the offending Rh factor antigen. Such action causes the formation of clumps in the blood that can create a stoppage that will result in death.

As with all allergies, the first exposure may not cause a serious reaction because of the time required for the body to form anti–bodies. A second transfusion or pregnancy, however, when the antibodies are already present in the blood and the immune system is ready to produce more, will almost always cause severe complications.

Careful typing of blood and the development of a substance that disables the Rh antibodies have made complications from Rh incompatibility relatively rare.

rickets A deficiency disease of children that often causes bone deformity. Those who contract rickets tend to exhibit swollen joints or distortion of limbs and other deformities caused by softened and irregular bone growth that is the result of insufficient vitamin D to aid in the absorption of calcium and its merging into bone.

Vitamin D is formed in the skin from exposure to sunlight

and is available in the diet in dairy products and in fish oils. A lack of winter sunlight to aid in the formation of vitamin D can contribute to the deficiency.

rigor mortis Stiffening of the muscles after death.

ringworm A contagious, fungal infection of the skin. Ringworm often appears as round patches that leave red rings; hence, its name. Ringworm may appear in a variety of forms and on various areas of the body. Athlete's foot is a type of ringworm.

The fungus is transmitted by contact with an infected person or contaminated object, such as clothing, a towel, or a hair brush. Such personal items should be cleaned with a detergent to prevent spread of the infection.

Although ringworm is more of an inconvenience than a threat, it is similar to skin infections that may be more serious and therefore should be referred to a physician.

Rocky Mountain spotted fever An infectious disease transmitted by wood ticks. The microorganism that causes Rocky Mountain spotted fever is a parasite harbored by small animals, such as, dogs, rabbits, chipmunks, squirrels, etc., from which it is spread to man.

Despite its name, the disease is not limited to the Rocky Mountain area, but occurs in other parts of the world as well. Infection produces chills and fever, painful muscles and joints, and skin eruptions.

rosacea A chronic disease characterized by reddening of the facial skin and often accompanied by pustules.

In severe cases, the nose may become red, swollen, and marked by large pores and blood vessels near the surface of the skin. Cause of the condition is uncertain, but it has been linked to excessive consumption of caffeine in coffee, tea, cola, etc., and to alcohol.

rubella A mild, contagious, viral infection; German measles. The onset of is characterized by a runny nose, swollen glands in the neck, and a low grade fever. Small red spots become visible on the face and neck within a few days, then quickly disappear as the rash spreads over the entire body. The second rash also lasts a few days, but swelling of the glands may persist for a bit longer.

The most serious problem associated with rubella is the likelihood of birth defects if the virus has been contracted during pregnancy.

rubeola See ***measles***

rupture To break open; that which has broken open, as a tearing of tissue; a ***hernia***.

salmonella A bacterium that is the cause of a type of food poisoning. Salmonella is generally contracted by eating foods, such as meat, chicken, or eggs, that have been contaminated. The condition causes cramps, nausea and diarrhea. Although generally mild, lasting only a few days, salmonella can be extremely serious in the very young, the elderly, or one who is already ill. Such cases should be referred to a physician promptly.

sarcoma Any of a number of malignant tumors that originate in connective tissue, such as bone or muscle.

scabies A contagious skin disease caused by a burrowing mite. Intense itching is induced by the mite burrowing into the skin to lay her eggs, generally in the area of the wrist, fingers, genitals or feet.

Medication can relieve itching and promote healing. The disease may be spread by close contact; anyone associating with an infested person should be treated as well.

scarlet fever A highly contagious bacterial infection. Scarlet fever is named for a characteristic scarlet rash covering the body that accompanies a fever and sore throat. The condition is customarily treated with antibiotics, bed rest, and a diet that contains lots of fluids.

scar tissue Connective tissue that has formed to replace normal tissue damaged by disease or injury.

schizophrenia A type of mental illness characterized by withdrawal from reality. Schizophrenia generally begins in adolescents or young adults, and may be evidenced by withdrawal, hallucinations, or discussions with a nonexistent third party with references to the subject as though he or she were not there.

sciatica Severe pain in the lower back extending along the path followed by the sciatic nerve down the length of the back of the thigh.

scoliosis Abnormal curvature of the spine. Usually, the condition occurs late in life, resulting from disease of the bones or muscles supporting the spinal column; however, it may be a congenital malformation of the vertebrae that can be corrected, at least in part, by surgery.

scurvy A disease caused by vitamin C deficiency. Vitamin C is especially important in forming connective tissue that seals wounds, activation of enzymes important to healing, and the prevention of clotting.

Serious symptoms of scurvy such as anemia, general weakness, and internal hemorrhaging attributed to a vitamin C deficiency are rare today, but more obvious ones such as bleeding gums and slow healing are not. Vitamin C cannot be synthesized by the body, nor is it stored in the body. It is often destroyed by other substances, such as medications or drugs; therefore, it should be a regular part of the diet or a dietary supplement.

sebaceous cyst A swelling formed by the retention of sebum when the duct of a sebaceous gland is obstructed. The sebaceous glands secrete sebum, an oily substance that aids in protecting the skin. A gland that continues to produce sebum when the duct is blocked, fills and becomes distended with the substance. Frequently the cyst will infect, burst, and expel its contents; one that does not burst can be surgically removed.

seizure A sudden attack of any kind, as by an epileptic fit, heart attack, convulsions, or a stroke.

senility A condition that describes the infirmities of old age. *Senility* may be used to depict the condition of being old, but is more often used to express infirmities, especially a decline in mental faculties such as memory lapse, slowed speech, lethargy, lack of ability to perform routine tasks, loss of appetite, anxiety, insensitivity to others, irritability, or withdrawal. Severe mental decline may be manifest in impulsive or inappropriate behavior, incontinence, inability to walk, etc.

In general, these conditions are progressive, that is, once begun, they continue to worsen, a decline that may be rapid or extended over a period of many years.

septic Descriptive of that in which bacteria or some other infectious substance is present.

shingles A painful viral infection of the nerves; *herpes zoster*. Caused by the same virus as chicken pox, shingles is characterized by itching, painful blistering along the course of the infected nerve. Treatment for shingles involves mainly medication to reduce the pain, and warm baths to bath the skin and prevent infection.

shock The effects of inadequate circulation of blood throughout the body. Shock is caused by the failure of the *cardiovascular system* which circulates blood to provide an adequate supply to every part of the body.

For more detailed information, see the ***FIRST AID GUIDE,*** *Shock.*

SIDS See ***crib death***

sigmoidectomy Surgical removal of the final section of the large intestine that connects to the rectum.

sinusitis Inflammation of the sinuses, cavities in the bones of the face that are lined with mucous membrane.

Normally, the sinuses are kept clear by draining into the nasal passages, but if there is any obstruction to the passage of mucus, they may become infected.

Commonly, sinusitis is associated with congestion from allergies, cold, or flu, but infection may also be caused by injury, swimming, or an abscessed tooth. Symptoms vary, but are often similar to cold or flu: congestion, chills, fever, sore throat, and headache. For some sufferers, most incapacitating is a characteristic, severe headache. The sinus itself may appear puffy and swollen, and be tender to the touch.

Medication and moist heat are most effective for promoting drainage to relieve the pressure and remove the source of the infection. In extreme or chronic cases, surgery may be necessary to correct the condition.

keleton The framework of bone that serves to support the softer body parts.

For a more detailed description, see the ***FIRST AID GUIDE***, *A Short Course in Anatomy*.

kin The external covering of the body.

For a more detailed description, see the ***FIRST AID GUIDE***, *A Short Course in Anatomy*.

leep A natural state of rest characterized by a lack of voluntary thought or movement.

During sleep, the body passes through a number of alternating states between that of being almost awake and of REM, or rapid eye movement, that is deep sleep. It is during REM sleep, so named because of the characteristic erratic movements of the eyeballs, that dreams occur.

slipped disk Displacement of the disk of cartilage between the vertebrae; *herniated disk*; *ruptured disk*.

smallpox A highly contagious viral disease. Smallpox is characterized by high fever and the emergence of red spots, first on the face and then spreading to the entire upper body. After a day or two, the spots become pu tules that may leave pockmarks on the face or neck. Although once a leading causes of death throughout th world, smallpox has been virtually eradicated.

smell Descriptive of the function of the olfactory nerves. To detect odor or aroma.

sneeze An involuntary action characterized by a sudder forcible emission of air through the nose and mouth; protective mechanism for expelling irritants.

spasm The sudden, involuntary contraction of a muscl that may be repeated for a time.

speech The ability to create unique sounds for the sol purpose of communicating thought.

sphygmomanometer Any device used for measurin blood pressure.

The most common sphygmomanometer is a device wit an inflatable cuff that is wrapped around the arm and gauge to indicate pressure. The cuff is inflated to stop th flow of blood through the artery, then gradually deflate so that the physician can determine the pressure at whic the first pulse is heard and, as the cuff continues to de flate, the pressure at which the stream of blood passin through the artery is heard. Normal adult pressure i about 120/80 although some variance from that standar is not abnormal. Both readings are of value to the physi cian in making a diagnosis.

spinal column The spinal column, or backbone, is mad up of thirty-three segments that are composed of ***verte brae*** joined by strong ***ligaments*** and ***cartilage*** to form flexible column that encloses the ***spinal cord***.

spinal cord The network of nerve tissue that extend through the spinal column. Nerves leaving the brair connect to the spinal cord, pass down through the spina column, the opening in the center of the spine, anc branch off to all parts and organs of the body. There are mainly two types of nerves entering and leaving the spinal cord: *sensory nerves* that convey sensations such as heat, cold, pain, and touch from different parts of the body to the brain; and *motor nerves* that convey impulses from the brain to the muscles causing movement.

spine The human spine, consisting of 29 bones called *vertebrae* that provide the basis of a firm, flexible frame for the trunk of the body, and that encases the spinal cord and its nerve roots. The spinal vertebrae are separated and protected from each other by disks of cartilage that absorb the impact of stress, as in walking or running.

spleen An abdominal organ that has several functions, primarily those of removing worn out or abnormal blood cells from circulation and the manufacture of antibodies.

sporadic Recurring at irregular intervals.

sporotrichosis A chronic infection caused by a fungus that exists in soil and decaying vegetation. Sporotrichosis commonly enters the body through ingestion or inhalation. The infection is usually limited to eruptions on the skin, but may involve the lymph glands.

sprain An injury due to stretching or tearing ligaments or other tissues at a joint.

For more detailed information, see the ***FIRST AID GUIDE***, *Sprains, Strains, and Fractures.*

spur A pointed outgrowth on a bone, caused by illness or injury.

sputum Saliva, often mixed with other material, as mucus, that is spit from the mouth. Excess mucus in the respiratory tract, usually the result of irritation or infection, stimulates nerve endings that set up a cough reflex to eject the offending material.

stammer To involuntarily hesitate or falter when speaking. The condition is usually overcome by speech therapy that focuses on relaxation and proper breathing.

sterilization Any condition that inhibits reproductive capability, caused by disease, disability or surgery.

In men, surgical sterilization is called a vasectomy, a relatively simple procedure that involves cutting through the tubes that carry sperm from the testes to the urethra.

In women, the most common procedure is cutting or blocking the fallopian tubes that carry the egg from the ovaries to the uterus.

sternum See ***breastbone.***

stimulant Anything that has the effect of increasing the activity of a process or organ.

stomach The digestive organ located between the esophagus that delivers ingested food and the duodenum, the first part of the small intestine. The stomach churns food and mixes it with digestive juices before passing it to the duodenum for digestion and absorption.

strain An injury to a muscle or a tendon caused by stretching or overexertion.

For more detailed information, see the ***FIRST AID GUIDE****, Sprains, Strains, and Fractures.*

strangulation Constriction that cuts off a vital flow, as of air to the lungs or blood to an organ.

strep throat A bacterial infection of the throat. Strep throat may cause chills and fever, and swelling of the lymph glands.

stress Any force or influence that tends to distort the normal physical or mental state. Physically, stress is produced by normal body action, as on joints and ligaments when walking or running, or by abnormal stimulation, such as disease or injury. Mentally or emotionally, some stress is inherent in every conscious thought or decision. It is recognized as a harmful condition, however, when it is sufficiently intense as to be beyond the ability of the body's regulating mechanisms to cope with it.

Stress is brought on by conditions that vary with the individual. For most, major lifetime events, such as job loss or death of a loved one may create an extreme response that brings on or worsens a mental or physical disorder. Others overreact to lesser events, as an adolescent who suffers asthma attacks before examinations in school.

stricture An abnormal constricting of a passage that prevents normal function.

stroke The sudden disruption of blood supply to an area of the brain; *apoplexy*. The consequence of a stroke is the loss of function in those areas of the body controlled by the affected area of the brain.

For more detailed information, see the ***FIRST AID GUIDE***, *Medical Emergencies*.

sty A common infection of the sebaceous gland of the eyelash. The oil–secreting gland may become infected and pass the infection on to the hair follicle to which it is attached. The infection causes redness, swelling, and often, tenderness in the area. Eventually, the sty may mature and burst, expelling its contents.

A sty will normally run its course without special treatment. Discomfort may be eased with occasional warm compresses and by wearing dark glasses. A child with a sty should be cautioned against touching or rubbing the eye and warned of the possibility that matter from the eye may dry during sleep, making the eyelid difficult to open on awakening—a frightening experience. The dry matter is easily dissolved with a warm, moist compress.

subconscious Descriptive of those mental processes that occur without conscious recognition or with reduced perception, as those that are instinctive or reactive.

subdural hematoma A blood clot in the skull, beneath the outer covering of the brain

sublimation The suppression of base instincts to adapt to socially acceptable behavior.

subliminal Descriptive of that which is below the level of consciousness.

sudden death The immediate and unexpected cessation of respiration and functional circulation.

For more detailed information, see the ***FIRST AID GUIDE***, *Artificial Ventilation.*

sudden infant death syndrome See ***crib death***

suffocation Any condition that inhibits the flow of air into the lungs.

suicide The conscious taking of one's own life.

sunburn Inflammation and discoloration of the skin from excessive exposure to the ultraviolet rays of the sun. Despite the extreme discomfort, most need only be treated with applications of medicated ointment to restore moisture balance in the skin. Extreme cases, however, involve serious damage to skin and loss of body moisture.

Any sunburn victim who suffers from chills, fever, or nausea should be placed in the care of a physician. Regular exposure to the ultraviolet rays of the sun has been linked to cancer and other skin diseases; therefore, one who is regularly subject to such exposure should consider the use of a sun blocking lotion for protection.

superficial Near the surface; descriptive of that which expresses only limited intrusion, as a superficial wound.

suppurative Descriptive of the formation or presence of pus, as in a wound.

suture To join together the edges of an open wound by stitching; the stitch used to join the edges of a wound.

symptom A characteristic indicator of a disease or infection, either evident to the examiner or a sensation described by the subject, that, taken with other indicators, forms the basis for a diagnosis.

syncope Loss of consciousness caused by a temporary interruption in the flow of blood to the brain; fainting.

syndrome A number of indicators that, taken together, form a pattern for diagnosis.

synesthesia The alteration or transference of impressions from one sense to another, commonly that of smell or taste perceived as a visual color image.

synovial fluid The fluid present in the joints to lubricate the synovial membrane.

synovial membrane The membrane of joints that, with synovial fluid, reduces friction between joined bones.

tachycardia Abnormally rapid heartbeat, caused by disease, medication, drugs, exercise, or emotional distress.

tantrum Uncontrollable rage or temper.

tapeworm A long, thin, flat worm that survives in the intestinal tract. Tapeworms can cause weight loss and anemia in spite of a healthy appetite

taste That one of the senses stimulated by contact with the taste buds in the mouth. Basically, the taste buds allow one to distinguish among four different characteristics—sweet, sour or acid, salty, and bitter. The distinctive taste of a specific substance is a combination of the sensory perception of the taste buds, its aroma, and its texture.

tendinitis Inflammation of a tendon. Although tendinitis may be associated with disease, it is most usually the result of physical activity. One who engages in athletics or physical labor without proper conditioning or preparation is a candidate for a variety of injuries, including tendinitis. Tendinitis is manifested in pain and tenderness of the affected area and is usually relieved by resting.

tendon The tough, fibrous connective tissue by which muscle is joined to bone.

teratoma A tumor comprised of embryonic tissue.

tetanus An infectious disease associated with severe

muscle contraction; lockjaw. Tetanus bacteria enter the body through an open wound and produce a toxin that commonly infects the muscles of the jaw, producing contractions that cause the jaw to become fixed in a tightly closed position. The disease may affect other muscles and, in some cases, contractions are extremely painful. The disease may be treated with drugs to counteract the infection and others to relax the muscles. Prevention requires prompt cleansing of puncture wounds and immunization with the tetanus vaccine.

tetany A disease caused by lack of calcium in the blood. Tetany is commonly associated with parathyroid disease or a lack of vitamin D. The condition causes muscle spasms and violent twitching, especially of extremities.

thalamus A part of the brain involved in the transmission of sensory messages.

therapeutics The branch of medicine concerned with the treatment of disease.

thermography A technique for determining variance in temperature with the aid of an infrared camera. Infrared rays from a source vary with the amount of heat given off. An infrared camera can thus produce an image showing relative amounts of heat, allowing a diagnostician to detect areas of abnormal growth or activity.

thiamine See ***vitamin B complex***

thirst An intuitive desire for fluid. The need is signaled by a dry feeling in the throat and mouth as moisture evaporates rapidly from those areas when the body lacks water. In order to maintain normal function, the body needs constant replenishment of fluids to replace those lost through the action of the lungs, sweat glands and kidneys. A number of conditions, such as stress, heavy exercise, or hemorrhage or disease can increase the need.

thoracotomy A surgical opening of the chest, or thorax,

for diagnostic purposes or for corrective surgery.

thrombocyte See ***platelet***

thrombosis Coagulation of blood; the process of forming a blood clot in the heart or a blood vessel.

thrombus A blood clot that forms in the heart or a blood vessel.

thrush A fungal infection, most often affecting children, that is characterized by the formation of white patches and ulcers on the mouth and throat.

thymus A lymph gland located in the upper part of the chest cavity, or thorax; the thymus gland.

thyroid gland A gland located in front of the throat that secretes hormones for regulating the body's development and metabolism. Thyroid hormone is involved in a number of processes throughout the body, such as regulation of body temperature, growth, fertility, and the conversion of food to energy.

tic An intermittent, involuntary spasm or twitch, usually of the facial muscles.

tick Any of a number of parasitic mites that feed on the blood of their host. Ticks attach themselves to the skin of humans and animals, carrying and transmitting a number of diseases, such as Rocky Mountain spotted fever.

To avoid further damage to tissue and risk of infection, a tick should not be pulled or rubbed off; removal is best accomplished by covering it with salad oil or by touching it with a lighted cigarette that will cause it to back off.

tinnea See ***ringworm***

tinnitus A buzzing or ringing in the ear. Tinnitus may be caused by blockage of the Eustachian tubes, excessive wax in the ears, or a disorder of the auditory nerves.

tissue Any of a number of distinctive materials, comprised of like cells, that make up the structures of the body, such as *connective tissue*.

tonsillectomy A surgical procedure for the removal of the tonsils.

tonsillitis Infection or inflammation of the tonsils, two small, lymph glands located on each side of the throat at the back of the mouth. Tonsillitis is usually evidenced by a sore throat, fever and difficulty in swallowing. Often there is evidence of swelling and inflammation of the organ. Treatment generally involves rest, relieving symptoms, and sometimes, antibiotics. Tonsils are seldom surgically removed except in extreme conditions.

topical Descriptive of that designated for a particular part of the body, as the applying of a medication.

torso The trunk of the human body.

torticollis Wryneck; a contraction of the muscles on one side of the neck that causes the neck to twist and the head to incline to one side.

toxemia A condition in which toxins are in the blood and thereby spread throughout the system.

toxin Any of a variety of matter produced by microorganisms that cause infection and disease in humans.

trachea The tube that extends from the larynx to the bronchi in the respiratory tract; the windpipe.

tracheotomy A surgical incision in the front of the neck into the trachea. A tracheotomy is performed when injury or disease causes obstruction in the windpipe or makes it necessary to remove the larynx.

transplant To transfer an organ or tissue; the organ or tissue so transferred. Transplants range from those of the cornea of the eye, to skin grafts, to those of organs and tissues, many yet in the experimental stage.

The overriding problem with transplants is one of rejection—the body's immune system builds antibodies to destroy the unfamiliar tissue—so that immunosuppressive drugs are necessary to suspend this reaction. The danger in the use of such drugs as they make the body vulnerable to other infection.

The cornea carries no blood and poses no threat; grafting skin from one part to another of the same body poses no threat. One of the more common transplants, that of a kidney, is most successful when the donor is a close relative who most nearly matches the tissue of the recipient.

The transplant of other organs, such as the heart, liver, or pancreas, have had mixed results as have artificial devices, and even organs or tissue from other species. Undoubtedly, there will be failures, but as knowledge increases there will be rewarding successes.

trauma A sudden affliction, either physical or psychological. In the practice of medicine, *trauma* is generally descriptive of physical injury or the physical symptoms of ***shock.*** In psychiatry, it describes a distressing emotional experience that is difficult for the subject to deal with, and that may produce a lasting effect, as a neurosis.

tremor An involuntary shaking of a part of the body.

triage A system of assigning a priority to the treatment of victims in a medical emergency based on such factors as urgent need and the chance for survival.

trunk The main part of the human body excepting the ***head*** and the ***extremities***. The trunk is divided into upper and lower parts by a muscular partition known as the ***diaphragm***. The upper portion of the trunk is the ***chest***, its cavity, and organs. The lower part of the trunk is the ***abdomen***, its cavity, and organs.

tuberculosis A bacterial infection characterized by the formation of tubercles. The body's immune system cannot destroy the bacterium that cause tuberculosis; therefore it encloses them in small nodules called tubercles. As a result, the invading organism remains in the body, although it is prevented from causing infection.

Most infected by tuberculosis will not experience symptoms, as the bacteria remain dormant in the body. Of those who do experience symptoms, not all will do so immediately after being infected. In many cases, the tuberculosis lies dormant and becomes active only when the body is weakened by some other disease.

Tuberculosis usually acts on the lungs, but it can infect other parts of the body, such as kidneys, spine, or digestive tract. Tuberculosis is contagious, spread by bacteria from the coughing or sneezing of an infected person. Anyone in contact with a tuberculosis sufferer should consult a physician for testing.

Symptoms of tuberculosis are not distinctive from other infections—in the early stages, they involve fever, fatigue and weight loss; later there may be chest pains, shortness of breath and spots of blood in coughed up sputum—any sign of blood in the lungs should be referred to a physician regardless of the suspected cause.

tumor Any growth of new tissue that is independent of its surroundings. A tumor may be ***benign*** or ***malignant.***

turgid Descriptive of that which is swollen or abnormally distended.

ulcer An erosion, or open sore. Ulcers may occur as ***bedsores*** on the lower back, as sores of the feet or legs associated with diabetes or varicose veins, in the digestive tract such as a ***peptic ulcer***, etc.

ultrasound The use high frequency sound waves to record an image of internal tissue that cannot be detected by X rays. The sound waves are focused into beams that are deflected differently by tissues of varying density so that the existence and position of the tissue can be recorded to produce a visual image. Ultrasound is a valuable tool in detection and diagnosis, such as the formation and position of gallstones, or irregularities in blood vessels. It can also be used for examination of a fetus during pregnancy, as it produces no harmful emission of radiation.

undulant fever See ***brucellosis***

urinary bladder The organ or sac that receives, holds, and discharges urine.

urology The branch of medicine that deals with the study, diagnosis and treatment of diseases and disorders of the urinary tract and reproductive system.

urticaria An allergic condition characterized by itchy blotches or welts; hives. Urticaria may be caused by allergens in food, as tomatoes, strawberries, etc.; certain drugs; bacteria; animal hair; or the environment, as exposure to cold or the sun. An outbreak may last less than an hour or continue for weeks, often subsiding, then reappearing from time to time. A mild attack is merely annoying, but more serious attacks may be accompanied by fever or nausea and even difficulty in breathing if the respiratory tract is infected. Treatment generally involves administering antihistamines.

varicose veins A condition characterized by swollen, knotted blood vessels, usually in the legs.

Veins in the legs have a special valve to keep the blood returning to the heart from running backward. A vein weakened from obesity, lack of exercise, or long stretches of sitting or standing, may stretch and the valves not allowed to close properly. Blood then leaks backward and gathers in pools that further weaken the vein.

Varicose veins may be temporary, as in the case of pregnancy. In such cases, resumption of normal activity and exercise may help them to return to normal.

The condition is obvious, as it develops close to the skin and appears as twisting, bulging lines that run down the legs, often with dark blue spots or sections. Often the ankles swell and the skin in the affected area becomes dry and itchy. In severe cases there may be shooting pains and cramps, especially at night.

Varicose veins are not serious in themselves, but they may allow the formation of clots or inflammation that can cause a more serious problem.

vein Any of the numerous vessels that carry blood back to the heart

vertebrae The bones or segments that make up the spinal column and through which the spinal cord passes. *Vertebrae* is plural; *vertebra* is singular.

vertigo A disorder in which dizziness is accompanied by a sensation of moving and the feeling that one's surroundings are moving as well.

virulent Descriptive of that which can overcome the body's defenses and cause infection.

Of a disease or poisonous substance that is powerful and rapid in its advance, or malignant.

virus A parasite that attacks plants, animals, and bacteria; typically, a disease caused by a virus.

vitamin Any of a number of organic substances that are essential for the normal growth and functioning of the body. Most vitamins are derived from various food sources and some are synthesized in the body.

vitamin A Obtained primarily from green leafy vegetables, eggs, butter, milk, liver, and fish liver oils, vitamin A is essential to proper formation of cells of the skin and mucous membranes, and for night vision.

vitamin B complex

B vitamins are divided into several constituents:

Thiamine, or *Vitamin* B_1 is available mainly in yeast, whole grain, meat, eggs, and potato; important to promote growth and in the proper functioning of nerves.

Riboflavin, or *Vitamin* B_2 may be obtained from milk, eggs, cheese, liver, and meats; it promotes growth and aids in the body cells' metabolism.

Vitamin B_6 is contained in whole grains, fish, liver, and yeast. It is important in the metabolism of protein and the production of antibodies to fight infection.

Vitamin B_{12} is available from milk, eggs, liver and meat. It is important in the metabolism of fat and sugar; in the production of blood; and for normal growth and neurological function.

Niacin, or *nicotinic acid*, that is obtainable from yeast, liver, meat, and whole grains, aids in the metabolism of sugar and is vital to proper function of the intestines.

Folic acid, obtained from green leafy vegetables, giblets, and liver, aids in the metabolism of sugar and amino acids, the components of protein.

Pantothenic acid, obtainable from green leafy vegetables and meat, is essential to cell growth.

Biotin, found in yeast, egg and liver is essential for normal growth.

Choline, found in green leafy vegetables and meat, is essential to the metabolism of fat.

Inositol, from green leafy vegetables and meat, is linked to the metabolism of cholesterol

Vitamin C Vitamin C, or *ascorbic acid* is obtained mainly from citrus fruit, such as oranges, lemons or grapefruit, and from potatoes or tomatoes. Vitamin C is vital to the function of blood vessels, healing and the production of connective tissue.

Vitamin D Found mainly in fish liver oil and in fortified milk, vitamin D can also be formed on the skin from sunlight. It is essential to the metabolism of calcium and important to normal formation of teeth and bones.

Vitamin E Obtained from cold-pressed oils, wheat germ and whole grains, vitamin E is linked to a number of functions in the body including the manufacture of blood and to fertility.

Vitamin K Available from leafy green vegetables and fish, vitamin K is necessary for the blood to clot normally.

vitiligo A condition in which there is an absence of natural pigment in sections of the skin or hair that appear as whitish or light patches.

vomit To expel the contents of the stomach forcibly through the mouth.

wart A small, dry growth on the skin. A wart is not malignant nor, in most cases, harmful in any other way. The condition is caused by a virus that produces enlargement of the cells of the skin.

wean To teach a baby to consume foods other than mother's milk or formula.

wheeze Difficulty in breathing that is accompanied by a whistling sound.

whooping cough An infectious disease of the respiratory system that affects the mucous membranes lining the air passages. Primarily a disease of children, it is characterized by a series of coughs followed by an intake of breath that causes a whooping sound.

x rays, X rays High frequency electromagnetic radiation capable of penetrating some solid objects, of destroying tissue by extended exposure, and of creating an image on a photographic plate or a fluorescent screen. X rays are used to create images for study and diagnosis.

yellow fever An often fatal viral infection contracted by the bite of an infected mosquito. Yellow fever attacks the liver and kidneys, and causes chills, fever, jaundice, and internal hemorrhaging.

yellow jaundice See ***jaundice***

zoonosis Any disease in animals that can be transmitted to man.

zoster Herpes zoster. See ***shingles.***

First Aid Guide

Contents

A Short Course in Anatomy 113
General Procedures 123
Artificial Ventilation 127
Cardiopulmonary Resuscitation 139
Controlling Bleeding 149
Shock 157
Treating Wounds 163
Burns and Scalds 189
Sprains, Strains, and Fractures 195
Transporting the Injured 225
Environmental Emergencies 233
Medical Emergencies 239

Importance of First Aid

Sudden illness or injury can often be serious unless proper care is administered promptly. **First aid** is immediate attention to one suffering from illness or injury.

First aid does not replace the physician, but assists the victim until proper medical assistance can be obtained. One of the most important principles of first aid is to obtain medical assistance in all cases of serious injury. Even seemingly minor injuries should be examined by a physician if there is any question of proper treatment or possibility of complication.

The urgent need for quick action in responding to life–threatening situations makes it important for everyone to be able to give proper emergency care until a victim can be transported to a medical facility.

When first aid is properly administered, it can often restore natural breathing and circulation, control bleeding, reduce the severity of shock, protect injuries from infection or other complications, and help conserve the victim's strength. If prompt steps are taken and medical aid is obtained, the victim's chances of recovery are greatly improved.

The principal aims of first aid are:

- ✓ Relief of life–threatening conditions
- ✓ Protection from further injury and complications
- ✓ Arrangement of transportation for the victim to a medical facility in such a manner as not to complicate the injury or subject the victim to unnecessary discomfort
- ✓ Making the victim as comfortable as possible to conserve strength

First aiders must be able to take charge of a situation, keep calm while working under pressure, and organize others to do likewise. By demonstrating competence and using well–selected words of encouragement, first aiders should win the confidence of others nearby and do everything possible to reassure the apprehensive victim.

During the first few minutes following an injury, the injured person has a better chance of full recovery if there is someone nearby trained in first aid. Everyone should be able to give effective assistance until an injured person can receive professional medical care.

A Short Course in Anatomy

To grasp procedures and effectively administer first aid, it is necessary to know something about the anatomy (structure) and physiology (functions) of the body.

The body is composed of solids, such as bones and tissue; and fluids, such as blood, and the secretions of various glands, organs and membranes. The principal regions of the body are the head, neck, chest, abdomen, and the upper and lower extremities.

For the purposes of this book, the upper extremity from one shoulder to the elbow will be referred to as the upper arm or simply the arm. The portion from the elbow to the wrist will be called the forearm; the portion of the lower extremity from the hip to the knee will be called the thigh; and the portion from the knee to the ankle, the leg.

Skeleton

The human skeleton is composed of approximately two hundred bones, classified according to shape as long, short, flat, and irregular bones. The skeleton forms a strong flexible framework for the body. It supports and carries the soft parts, protects vital organs from injury, gives attachment to muscles and tendons, and forms joints to allow movement. There are three major divisions of the human skeleton: the head; the trunk or main part of the body; and the upper and lower extremities or limbs.

Head

The head is composed of twenty–two bones, eight that are closely united to form the skull, a bony case that encloses and protects the brain; fourteen other bones form the face. The only movable joint in the head is the lower jaw.

Trunk

The trunk is composed of fifty–four bones and divided into upper and lower parts by a muscular partition known as the diaphragm.

The upper portion of the trunk is the chest, its cavity, and organs. The spinal column, or backbone, is made up of thirty–three segments that are composed of vertebrae joined by strong ligaments and cartilage to form a flexible column that encloses the spinal cord. The chest is formed by twenty–four ribs, twelve on each side, that are attached in the back to vertebrae. The seven upper pairs of ribs are attached to the breastbone in front by cartilage. The next three pairs of ribs are attached in front by a common cartilage to the seventh rib instead of the breastbone. The lower two pairs of ribs, known as the floating ribs, are not attached in front.

The lower part of the trunk is the abdomen, its cavity, and organs. The pelvis is a basin–shaped bony structure at the lower portion of the trunk. The pelvis is below the movable vertebrae of the spinal column, which it supports, and above the lower limbs, upon which it rests. Four bones compose the pelvis, the two bones of the backbone and the wing–shaped hip bones on either side. The pelvis forms the floor of the abdominal cavity and provides deep sockets in which the heads of the thigh bones fit.

Extremities

The upper extremity consists of thirty–two bones. The collarbone is a long bone, the inner end of which is attached to the breastbone and the outer end is attached to the shoulder blade at the shoulder joint. The collarbone lies just in front of and above the first rib. The shoulder blade is a flat triangular bone which lies at the upper and outer part of the back of the chest and forms part of the shoulder joint. The arm bone extends from the shoulder to the elbow. The two bones of the forearm extend from the elbow to the wrist. There are eight wrist bones, five bones in the palm of the hand, and fourteen finger bones, two in the thumb and three in each finger.

The lower extremity consists of thirty bones. The thigh bone, the longest and strongest bone in the body, extends from the hip joint to the knee; its upper end is rounded to fit into the socket in the pelvis, and its lower end broadens out to help form part of the knee joint. This flat triangular bone can be felt in front of the knee joint. The two bones in the leg extend from the knee joint to the ankle. There are seven bones in the ankle and back part of the foot, five long bones in the front part of the foot, and fourteen toe bones.

Most fractures and dislocations occur to the bones and joints of the extremities.

Joints and Ligaments

Two or more bones coming together form a joint. There are three types of joints: immovable joints, such as those in the skull; joints with limited motion, such as those of the ribs and lower spine; and freely movable joints, such as the knee, ankle, elbow, etc.

Freely movable joints are those most commonly injured and of most concern in first aid. The ends of bones forming a movable joint are covered by cartilage.

The bones are held in place by strong white bands, called ligaments, extending from one bone to another and entirely around the joint. A smooth membrane that lines the end of the cartilage and the inside of the ligaments secretes a fluid that keeps the joints lubricated.

Muscles and Tendons

Bones, the framework of the body, are mostly covered with flesh and muscle tissue which give the body its shape and contour.

There are two types of muscles: voluntary muscles: those that are consciously controlled, such as muscles of the arms and legs; and involuntary muscles: those that are not consciously controlled, such as muscles of the heart and those that control digestion and breathing.

Strong, inelastic, fibrous cords called tendons attach the muscles to the bones. The muscles cause the bones to move by flexing or extending.

Skin

Although the outer layer of skin, or epidermis, is made up of layers of cells that primarily serve to protect, it also contains cells that determine skin color. The epidermis constantly changes; as new layers are formed, old ones are shed. The layer of skin below the epidermis is the dermis that contains the blood vessels, nerves, and specialized structures such as sweat glands, that help to regulate body temperature, and hair follicles. The fat and soft tissue layer below the dermis is called the subcutaneous.

The skin has many protective functions. It is watertight and keeps internal fluids in while keeping germs out. A system of nerves transmit information about pain, external pressure, heat, cold, and relative position of parts of the body.

The skin is one of the most important organs of the body. The loss of a large part of the skin will result in death unless it can be replaced. Skin often provides important information to the first aider concerning the victim's condition, such as pale, sweaty skin that may indicate shock.

Chest Cavity

The chest cavity is cone–shaped, formed by the upper part of the spinal column or backbone at the back, the ribs on the sides, and the ribs and breastbone in front. The diaphragm, a thin, muscular partition at the bottom of the chest cavity separates the chest cavity and the abdominal cavity. The diaphragm is dome–shaped and lower in the back than in the front.

The lungs and the heart occupy most of the chest cavity. The heart lies between the lungs in the center of the chest behind the breastbone. It is positioned slightly to the left side, making the left lung smaller than the right. In addition to the heart and the lungs, the chest cavity contains the esophagus or food pipe that extends from the back of the throat down through the diaphragm to the stomach, the trachea or windpipe that extends to the lungs, and several major blood vessels.

Abdominal Cavity

The abdominal cavity is in the lower portion of the trunk, formed by the lower portion of the backbone, the muscles in the back and abdominal muscles at the sides and front. The diaphragm forms the top of the cavity and the pelvic basin forms the bottom.

The abdomen contains several important organs: the liver in the upper right portion; the stomach and the spleen in the upper left portion; the small and large intestines in the lower portion; the kidneys, one on each side in the back; and the urinary bladder in the pelvic region. There are also major blood vessels and other organs in the abdominal cavity.

Excretory Systems

Several systems serve to eliminate waste products that enter the body or are formed within it. The residue of food taken into the digestive system, mainly indigestible materials, together with secretions from various glands emptying into the intestines, is gathered in the lower portion of the large intestine and eliminated through the rectum as feces.

Surplus water, carrying dissolved salts that are excess in

the system or form a waste product, is extracted by the kidneys, collected in the bladder, and expelled as urine.

Carbon dioxide and certain volatile products carried by the blood are exchanged in the lungs for oxygen and pass from the body in exhaled air.

The skin contains small organs known as sweat glands that range from 400 to 2,800 per square inch over different parts of the body These glands are important in eliminating heat, excess fluid, and dissolved waste products.

Life and health depend on the body giving off its waste. Interference with normal functioning of any of the excretory systems results in illness and may even cause death.

Respiratory System

Oxygen enters the body through respiration, the breathing process. Oxygen is essential; all living tissue depends on oxygen that is carried by the blood. Any interference with breathing causes oxygen depletion throughout the entire body. Knowledge of the respiratory system and the organs concerned with respiration will greatly aid in understanding artificial ventilation.

Breathing consists of two separate acts: inhalation, enlarging the chest cavity so air is drawn into the lungs; and exhalation, decreasing the size of the chest cavity so air is forced out of the lungs. During inhalation the ribs are raised and the arch of the diaphragm falls and flattens, increasing the capacity of the chest cavity, and causing air to enter. In exhalation, an act normally performed with slight muscular action, the ribs fall to their normal position, the arch of the diaphragm rises decreasing the capacity of the chest cavity, and air is forced out.

When air is taken into the lungs and forced out the air passes through the nose, throat, and windpipe. Air is warmed and moistened in the nose; moist hairs and mucous membrane filter out much of the dust and foreign matter in inhaled air.

The throat is a continuation of the nose and mouth. At its lower end are two openings, one in front of the other: the opening in front, the trachea or windpipe, leads to the lungs; the one behind, the esophagus or food pipe, leads to the stomach. At the top of the windpipe is a flap, the epiglottis, that closes over the windpipe during swallowing to keep food or liquid from entering.

As the windpipe extends into the chest cavity toward the lungs, it divides into the two bronchial tubes, one going to each lung. The lungs are two cone–shaped bodies that are soft, spongy, and elastic. Each lung is covered by a closed sac called the pleura. The inside of the lungs communicates freely with the outside air through the windpipe.

Within the lungs, the bronchial tubes branch out like limbs of a tree, until they become very small. The bronchial tubes end in a group of air cells (alveoli) resembling a very small bunch of grapes. Around each of the air cells is a fine network of small blood vessels or capillaries. Through the thin walls of the air cells, the blood in these capillaries exchanges carbon dioxide, other waste matter, and the by–products of tissue activity from the body for a supply of oxygen from air breathed in. The discarded carbon dioxide and waste matter leave the air cells in exhaled air.

During breathing, the chest muscles and diaphragm expand the chest cavity so that the air pressure within the chest cavity becomes less than that outside. Air rushes to balance the pressure, filling the lungs.

If any air gets through the chest wall or if the lung is punctured so that air from the outside can fill the chest cavity, the lungs will not fill. This is because the air pressure is equal outside and inside the chest cavity. Thus, no suction is created for inhaling.

Breathing is an act which usually is automatic and one over which a person exerts only a limited degree of control. At rest, a healthy adult breathes about fifteen times a minute and takes in twenty–five to thirty cubic inches of air per breath. Each breath moves about one–half liter (500 cc, or one pint) of air. During strenuous work, the breathing rate and amount inhaled may increase several times.

Circulatory System

The circulatory system, that carries blood to and from all parts of the body, consists of the heart and blood vessels. Through the blood vessels, blood is circulated throughout the body under pressure supplied by the pumping action of the heart.

Blood

Blood is composed of serum or plasma, red cells, white cells, and platelets. Plasma is a fluid that carries the blood cells and transports nutrients to all tissues. It also transports waste products resulting from tissue activity to the organs for excretion. Red cells give color to the blood and carry oxygen. White cells aid in defending the body against infection. Platelets are essential to the formation of the blood clots necessary to stop bleeding.

One–fifteenth to one–twelfth of the body weight is blood. A person weighing one hundred fifty pounds will have approximately ten to twelve pints of blood. If the tissues do not receive blood, they will die from lack of oxygen. The loss of two pints of blood by an adult, or eight to ten percent of the total contained in the body, usually is serious. The loss of three pints over a short time, one to two hours, may be fatal. The loss of four pints or more will require blood transfusions to prevent death. At certain points in the body, fatal hemorrhages may occur in a very short time. The cutting of the two principal blood vessels in the neck, the principal blood vessels in the arms, or the principal blood vessels in the thighs may cause hemorrhage that will prove fatal in one to three minutes or even less. Rupture of the main trunk blood vessels of the chest and abdomen may prove fatal in less than thirty seconds.

Loss of blood causes a state of physical shock. This occurs because there is insufficient blood flowing through the tissues of the body to provide food and oxygen. When a person is in shock, vital body functions slow. If the conditions causing shock are not reversed, death may occur.

Blood Vessels

Oxygenated blood is carried from the heart by a large artery called the aorta. Smaller arteries branch off from the aorta, and those arteries in turn branch off into still smaller arteries. These arteries divide and subdivide until they become very small, ending in threadlike vessels known as capillaries, which extend into all the organs and tissues.

After the blood has furnished the necessary nourishment and oxygen to the tissues and organs of the body, it takes on waste products, particularly carbon dioxide. The blood returns to the heart by a different system of blood vessels known as veins. The veins are connected with the arteries through the capillaries.

Very small veins join forming larger veins which in turn join until the very largest veins return the blood to the heart. Blood passing through the kidneys is cleared of nonvolatile waste products. The heart pumps the blood delivered to it by the veins into the lungs, where it flows through another network of capillaries. There, the carbon dioxide and other volatile waste products are exchanged for oxygen through the delicate walls of air cells. The blood is thereby oxygenated and ready to return to the heart, which recirculates it throughout the body.

The time taken for the blood to make one complete circulation of the body through miles and miles of blood vessels is approximately seventy–five seconds in an adult at rest.

Heart

The heart is a hollow, muscular organ about the size of a fist, lying in the lower central region of the chest cavity. By the heart's pumping action, blood is under pressure and in constant circulation throughout the body. In a healthy adult at rest, the heart contracts between sixty and eighty times a minute; in a child, eighty to a one hundred times per minute. The effect of these contractions can be noted by the pulse, a spurt of blood through an artery. The pulse is most easily felt over the carotid artery on either side of the neck.

General Procedures

No two situations requiring first aid are the same; however, the following procedures are generally applicable:

- ✓ Take charge or follow instructions! If you are first at the scene, instruct someone to obtain medical help and others to assist as directed. If you arrive after someone else has taken charge, do as you are asked.
- ✓ Secure the scene. Ask someone to remove or mark any hazards.
- ✓ If several people have been injured, decide upon priorities in caring for each of the victims.
- ✓ Make a primary survey of the victim.
- ✓ Care for life–threatening conditions.
- ✓ Make a secondary survey of victim.
- ✓ Care for all injuries in order of need.
- ✓ Keep the injured person or persons lying down.
- ✓ Loosen restrictive clothing if necessary.
- ✓ Cover victim to keep warm and dry.
- ✓ Keep onlookers away from the victim.
- ✓ When necessary, improvise first aid materials using whatever is available.
- ✓ Cover all wounds completely.
- ✓ Prevent air from reaching burned surfaces as quickly as possible by using a suitable dressing.
- ✓ Remove small, loose foreign objects from a wound by brushing away from the wound with a piece of sterile gauze.
- ✓ **Do not** try to remove embedded objects.
- ✓ Place a bandage compress and a cover bandage over an open fracture without undue pressure before applying splints.
- ✓ Support and immobilize fractures and dislocations.
- ✓ Except for lower jaw dislocations, leave the re-

duction of fractures or dislocations to a doctor.

- ✓ Unless absolutely necessary, never move a victim until fractures have been immobilized.
- ✓ Test a stretcher before use, and carefully place an injured person on the stretcher.
- ✓ Carry the victim on a stretcher, without any unnecessary rough movements.

Evaluating the Situation

First aiders should take charge with full recognition of their own limitations and, while caring for life–threatening conditions, direct others briefly and clearly as to exactly what they should do and how to secure assistance. Information should be gathered to determine the extent of the injuries. This information can be obtained from: friends, relatives or bystanders; what you are able to observe at the scene; the victim, if he or she is conscious; and what you observe about the victim

Patient Assessment

Primary Survey

Many conditions may be life–threatening, but three in particular require immediate action:

- Respiratory arrest
- Circulatory failure
- Severe bleeding

Respiratory arrest and/or circulatory failure can set off a chain of events that will lead to death. Severe and uncontrolled bleeding can lead to an irreversible state of shock in which death is inevitable. Death may occur in a very few minutes if an attempt is not made to help the victim in these situations. Before caring for lesser injuries, the first aider should follow the ABC method to check for life–threatening conditions:

A) Airways—Establish responsiveness, position the victim, and, to ensure adequate breathing, an open airway must be established and maintained. If there are no signs of breathing, artificial ventilation must be given immediately.
B) Bleeding—Make a careful and thorough check for any bleeding. Control serious bleeding.
C) Circulation—If a victim experiences circulatory failure, **a person *trained* in cardiopulmonary resuscitation** (CPR) should check for a pulse, and if none is detected, start CPR at once.

In making the primary survey, **do not** move the victim any more than is necessary. Rough handling or any unnecessary movement might cause additional pain and aggravate serious injuries that have not yet been detected.

Secondary Survey

When life–threatening conditions have been controlled, the secondary survey should begin. The secondary survey is a head–to–toe examination to check **carefully** for any additional unseen injuries that can cause serious complications. This is conducted by examining for the following:

- ✓ Neck – Examine for neck injury—tenderness, deformity, medical identification necklace, etc. Spine fractures, especially in the neck area may accompany head injuries. Gently feel and look for any abnormalities. If a spinal injury is suspected, stop the secondary survey until the head can be stabilized. Follow these same precautions for any suspected spinal injury.
- ✓ Head – Without moving the head, check for blood in the hair, scalp lacerations, and contusions. Gently feel for possible bone fragments or depressions in the skull. Loss of fluid or bleeding from the ears and nose is an indication of possible skull fracture.

- ✓ Chest – Check the chest for cuts, impaled objects, fractures, and penetrating (sucking) wounds by observing chest movement. When the sides are not rising together or one side is not moving at all, there may be lung and rib damage.
- ✓ Abdomen – Gently feel the abdominal area for cuts, penetrations, and impaled objects, observing for spasms and tenderness.
- ✓ Lower back – Feel for deformity and tenderness.
- ✓ Pelvis – Check for grating, tenderness, bony protrusions, and depressions in the pelvic area.
- ✓ Genital region – Check for any obvious injury.
- ✓ Lower extremities – Check for discoloration, swelling, tenderness and deformities which are sometimes present with fractures and dislocations. Paralysis in the legs indicates a fractured back.
- ✓ Upper extremities – Check for discoloration, swelling, tenderness, and deformities which are sometimes present with fractures and dislocations. Paralysis in the arms and legs indicates a fractured neck. Check for a medical identification bracelet.
- ✓ Back surfaces – Injuries underneath the victim are often overlooked. Examine for bony protrusions, bleeding, and obvious injuries.

If the victim is conscious, explain that you are going to perform the head–to–toe survey and inform him or her what you are going to do. Be reassuring at all times.

Besides being trained in proper first aid methods, all first aiders should know what first aid equipment is available at home, at work, in the car, etc. The equipment should be checked periodically.

Artificial Ventilation

At the top of the windpipe is a flap, the epiglottis, which closes over the windpipe during swallowing to keep food or liquid from entering it. When a person is unconscious, the flap may fail to respond; therefore, no solids or liquids should be given by mouth, since they may enter the windpipe and lungs and cause suffocation or serious complications. If an unconscious person is lying on his or her back, the tongue is apt to fall against the back of the throat and interfere with air reaching the lungs. Sometimes it may block the throat entirely.

When a person is unconscious or breathing with difficulty, the head–tilt/chin–lift maneuver should be used to open the airway. **This procedure is not recommended for a victim with possible neck or spinal injuries.**

Causes of Respiratory Arrest

The most common causes of respiratory arrest are overdoses of narcotics, electric shock, drowning, suffocation, poisonous gases, head injuries, and heart problems.

Electric shock

The chance of accidental contact with electrical current is a common hazard. Any electric current can be dangerous. Electricity can cause paralysis of nerve centers that control breathing and stop or alter the regular beat of the heart.

The symptoms of electric shock are sudden loss of consciousness, impairment or absence of respiration or circulation, weak pulse, and sometimes burns. Breathing may be so weak and shallow that it cannot be detected.

If the victim is still in contact with the current, rescue the victim at once, being careful not to come in contact with the current. Every second of delay in removing a person

from contact lessens the chance of resuscitation.
Start artificial ventilation or CPR at once, if necessary.

Drowning

Remove a victim of drowning from the water as quickly as possible. Begin artificial ventilation immediately without taking the time to remove water in the respiratory tract.

Drowning is a form of suffocation. The supply of air has been cut off completely by water or spasm of the larynx. This cutoff does not create an immediate lack of oxygen in the body. There is a small reserve in the lungs, in the blood and in some tissue that can sustain life for up to six minutes or longer at low temperatures. Because this reserve is exhausted relatively quickly, it is important to start artificial ventilation as soon as possible.

Suffocation

Symptoms of suffocation in an unconscious person are: the lips, fingernails, and ear lobes become blue or darker in color; the pulse becomes rapid and weak; breathing stops; and the pupils of the eyes become dilated. The cause may be a blocked windpipe preventing air from getting into the lungs. Artificial ventilation is of no value until the blockage is removed.

Dangerous Gases

Several noxious or toxic gases encountered in everyday life can cause asphyxiation. These gases include carbon monoxide, sulfur dioxide, oxides of nitrogen, ammonia, hydrogen cyanide, and cyanogen compounds.

Persons should be aware of the early warning signs of exposure: headache, nausea, and tearing of the eyes are the three most common symptoms of the presence of dangerous gases. Rescuers should take care to protect themselves. Unless the surrounding air is good, take the victim to pure air immediately and begin artificial ventilation at once.

Nontoxic gases, such as carbon dioxide and methane, may also cause suffocation by displacing oxygen.

Principles of Artificial Ventilation

Artificial ventilation is the process for causing air flow in and out of the lungs when natural breathing has ceased or when it is very irregular or inadequate.

When breathing has ceased, the body's oxygen supply is cut off; brain cells start to die within four to six minutes. If artificial ventilation is started within a short time after respiratory arrest, the victim has a good chance for survival.

Certain general principles must always be kept in mind when administering artificial ventilation by any method:

- ✓ Time is of prime importance; every second counts.
- ✓ **Do not** take time to move the victim unless the accident site is hazardous.
- ✓ **Do not** delay ventilation to loosen the victim's clothing or warm the victim. These are of secondary importance to getting air into the victim's lungs.
- ✓ Perform head–tilt/chin–lift method for opening airway, which will bring the tongue forward.
- ✓ Remove visible foreign objects from the mouth.
- ✓ An assistant should loosen any tight clothing in order to promote circulation and go or send for help.
- ✓ Use a blanket, clothing or other material to keep the victim warm and dry.
- ✓ Maintain a steady, constant rhythm while giving artificial ventilation. Be sure to look for rise and fall of the chest and look, listen, and feel for return air. If none, look for upper airway obstruction.
- ✓ Continue artificial ventilation until one of the following occurs:
    - Spontaneous breathing resumes
    - You are relieved by a qualified person
    - A doctor pronounces the victim dead

- You are exhausted and unable to continue

✓ **Do not** fight the victim's attempts to breathe.

✓ Once the victim recovers, constantly monitor the condition because breathing may stop again.

✓ Keep the victim lying down.

✓ Treat the victim for physical shock.

Methods of Artificial Ventilation

The first thing to do when finding an unconscious person is to establish unresponsiveness by tapping on the shoulder and asking "Are you OK?" Place the victim on his or her back. Open the airway by using the head–tilt/chin–lift method. Remove any foreign objects from the mouth. To assess the presence or absence of spontaneous breathing in a victim, the rescuer should place his or her ear near the victim's mouth and nose while maintaining the open airway position. Look toward the victim's body and while observing the victim's chest, the rescuer should:

✓ **LOOK** for the chest to rise and fall;

✓ **LISTEN** for air escaping during exhalation;

✓ **FEEL** for the flow of air.

If the chest does not rise and fall and no air is heard or felt, the victim is not breathing. This assessment should take only three to five seconds. If it is determined that the victim is not breathing, begin artificial ventilation.

Mouth–to–Mouth Ventilation

Mouth–to–mouth ventilation is by far the most effective means of artificial ventilation for use on a victim of respiratory arrest.

✓ Open the airway. The most common cause of airway obstruction in an unconscious victim is the tongue. The tongue is attached to the lower jaw; moving the jaw forward lifts the tongue away from the back of the throat and opens the airway.

- Kneel at the victim's side with knee nearest the head opposite the victim's shoulders.
- Use the **head–tilt/chin–lift maneuver** (if no spinal injury exists) to open airway. Place one hand on the forehead and apply gentle, firm, backward pressure using the palm. Place the fingertips of your other hand under the chin. The fingertips are used to bring the chin forward and to support the jaw.

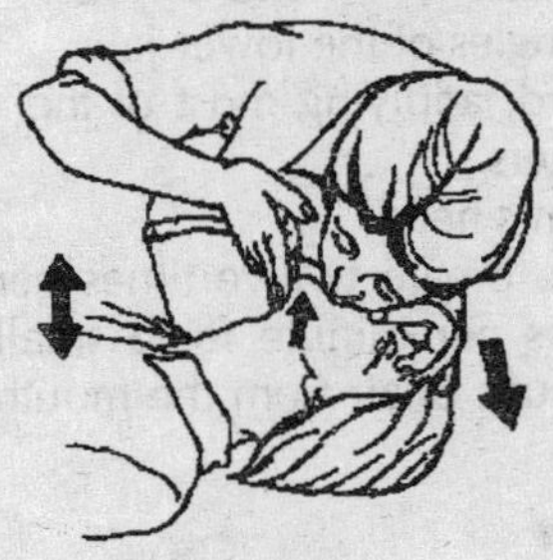

✓ Pinch the nose closed. Inhale deeply and place your mouth over the victim's mouth (over mouth and nose with children) making sure of a tight seal. Give two full breaths into the air passage watching for the chest to rise after each breath.

✓ Keep the victim's head extended at all times.

✓ Remove your mouth between breaths and let the victim exhale.

✓ Feel and listen for the return flow of air, and look for the fall of the victim's chest.

If neck injury is suspected, use modified jaw–thrust.

- ✓ Place victim on his or her back.
- ✓ Kneel at the top of victim's head, resting on your elbows.
- ✓ Reach forward and gently place one hand on each side of victim's chin, at the angles of the lower jaw.
- ✓ Push the victim's jaw forward, applying most of the pressure with your index fingers.
- ✓ **Do not** tilt or rotate the victim's head.

Repeat this procedure giving one breath twelve times per minute for an adult, fifteen times per minute for a small child. For an infant, give gentle puffs of air from the mouth twenty times per minute .

Mouth–to–Nose Ventilation

In certain cases, mouth–to–nose ventilation may be required. The mouth–to–nose technique is similar to mouth–to–mouth except that the lips are sealed by pushing the lower jaw against the upper jaw and air is forced into the victim by way of the nose.

Mouth–to–Stoma Ventilation

Persons who have undergone a laryngectomy (surgical removal of the larynx) have a permanent stoma (opening) that connects the trachea directly to the skin. The stoma is recognized as an opening at the front base of the neck. When such an individual requires rescue breathing, direct mouth–to–stoma ventilation is performed. The rescuer's mouth is sealed around the stoma, and air is blown into it until the chest rises. When the rescuer's mouth is removed from the stoma, permit the victim to exhale.

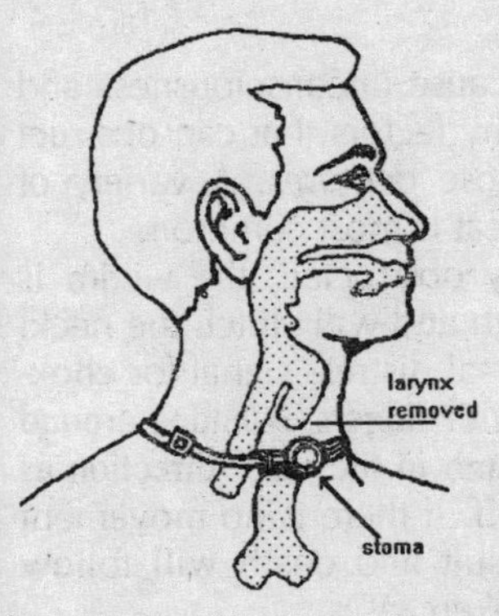

Other persons may have a temporary tracheostomy tube in the trachea. To ventilate these persons, seal the victim's mouth and nose by the rescuer's hand or by a tightly fitting face mask to prevent leakage of air when the rescuer blows into the tracheostomy tube.

Gastric Distention

One problem that may occur during artificial ventilation is the accumulation of air in the victim's stomach. Air in the stomach can cause two problems: reduction in the volume of air that enters the lungs because the diaphragm is farther forward than normal; and vomiting

To reduce distention, proceed as follows:

- ✓ Reposition the victim's head to provide a better airway.
- ✓ Limit ventilation force and volume.
- ✓ If vomiting occurs, turn the victim on his or her side if no spinal injury is present.
- ✓ **Do not** press on the stomach unless suction equip-

ment is available and you have been trained to use it, otherwise material from the stomach may become lodged in the lungs.

Obstructed Airway

Obstruction in the airway can cause unconsciousness and respiratory arrest. There are many factors that can obstruct the airway, such as gum or loose dentures. A variety of foods can cause choking, but meat is most common.

When the airway is completely obstructed, the victim is unable to speak, breath, or cough and will clutch the neck. Some people will use the universal distress signal for choking—a hand raised to the neck with fingers extended around the neck in one direction, the thumb in the other direction as though attempting to choke oneself. If there is no movement of air, unconsciousness will result and death will follow quickly if prompt action is not taken.

Conscious Victim, Sitting or Standing

- ✓ Determine if obstruction is partial or complete.
- ✓ If partial, encourage the victim to cough.
- ✓ If there is no air exchange, stand behind the victim and place your arms around the victim's waist.
- ✓ Grasp one fist in your other hand and position the thumb side of your fist against the middle of the victim's abdomen just above the navel and well below the rib cage.
- ✓ **Do not** squeeze victim.
- ✓ Press your fist into the victim's abdominal area with a quick upward thrust.
- ✓ Repeat the procedure if necessary.

Chest Thrust, Conscious Victim

The chest thrust is another method of applying the manual thrust when removing an obstruction. Use this method on a pregnant victim or when the rescuer is unable to wrap his or her arms around the victim's waist.

- ✓ When the conscious victim is standing or sitting, position yourself behind him or her and slide your arms under the armpits, so that you encircle the chest.
- ✓ Make a fist with one hand and place the thumb side of this fist on the victim's sternum.
- ✓ Make contact with the midline of the sternum about two to three finger–widths above the lower tip of the sternum.
- ✓ Grasp the fist with your other hand and press with a quick backward thrust.
- ✓ Repeat thrusts until the obstruction is expelled.

Victim Alone

The victim of an obstructed airway who is alone may use his or her own fist as described previously, or bend over the back of a chair and exert downward pressure.

Unconscious Victim

When you attempt to give artificial ventilation and you feel resistance, that is, the air is not getting in, the victim's airway is probably obstructed. The most common cause of airway obstruction in an unconscious person is the tongue falling back into the airway, which can be corrected by using the head–tilt/chin–lift maneuver. When the airway is obstructed by a foreign body, the obstruction must be cleared or ventilation will be ineffective.

Abdominal Thrust, Victim Lying Down

- ✓ Position victim on his or her back, face up.
- ✓ Straddle victim's hips, if possible.
- ✓ Place the heel of one hand against the middle of the victim's abdomen between the rib cage and the navel with fingers pointing toward the victim's chest.

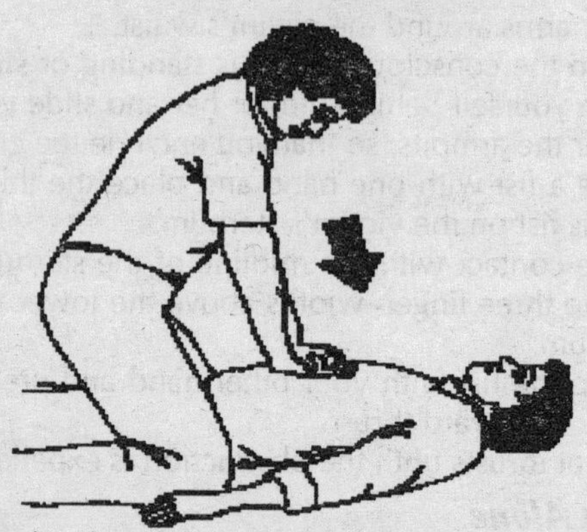

- ✓ Place other hand on top of the first.
- ✓ Move shoulders directly over the victim's abdomen.
- ✓ Press into the victim's abdominal area with a quick upward thrust.
- ✓ Do six to ten thrusts.
- ✓ Follow with opening mouth and finger sweep.
- ✓ Attempt artificial ventilation.
- ✓ Repeat the procedures until obstruction is cleared.

Chest Thrust, Victim Lying Down

Apply the chest thrust method to remove an obstruction from a pregnant or obese victim.

- ✓ Position the victim on his or her back.
- ✓ Open the airway.
- ✓ Kneel close to the victim.
- ✓ Place the heel of one hand on the lower half of the breast bone about one to one and one–half inches above the tip (xiphoid process) with fingers elevated. Heel of the hand must be parallel to the breast bone.
- ✓ Place the other hand on top of and parallel to the first hand.
- ✓ With shoulders directly over hands, exert a down-

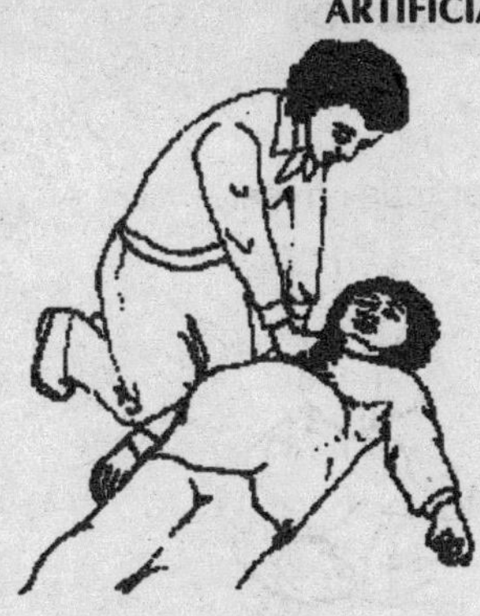

ward thrust. Keep elbows straight by locking them.

- ✓ Do six to ten thrusts.
- ✓ Follow with opening mouth and finger sweep.
- ✓ Attempt artificial ventilation.
- ✓ Repeat the procedure until obstruction is cleared.

Manual Removal

Whenever a foreign object is in the victim's mouth, remove it with the fingers. Manual thrusts may dislodge the obstruction, but not expel it. Turn the victim face up, open the mouth with the cross–finger technique or tongue–jaw lift, and clear the obstruction with a finger sweep.

Tongue–Jaw Lift

Open victim's mouth by grasping both the tongue and lower jaw and lifting.

Cross–Finger Technique

✓ Cross your thumb under your index finger.

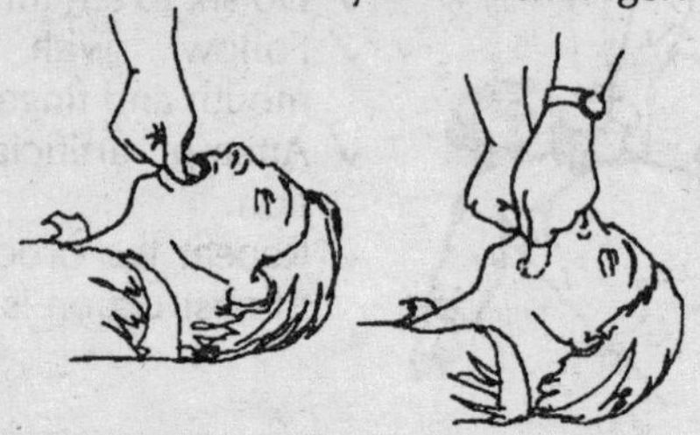

✓ Brace your thumb and finger against the victim's upper and lower teeth.

✓ Push your fingers apart to separate the jaws.

Finger Sweep

✓ Open the victim's jaws with one hand.

✓ Insert the index finger of your other hand down the inside of the cheek and into the throat to the base of the tongue.

✓ The index finger is then swept across the back of the throat in a hooking action to dislodge obstruction.

✓ Grasp and remove the foreign object when it comes within reach.

Cardiopulmonary Resuscitation (CPR)

Cardiopulmonary resuscitation (CPR) involves the use of artificial ventilation (mouth–to–mouth breathing) and external heart compression (rhythmic pressure on the breastbone). **These techniques must be learned through training and supervised practice. Courses are available through the American Heart Association and American Red Cross. Incorrect application of external heart compressions may result in complications such as damage to internal organs, fracture of ribs or sternum, or separation of cartilage from ribs.**

Application of cardiopulmonary resuscitation when not required could result in cardiac arrest, so never practice these skills on another person. When CPR is properly applied, the likelihood of complications is minimal and acceptable in comparison with the alternative—death.

Sudden Death

Sudden death is the **sudden** and **unexpected** cessation of respiration and functional circulation. *Sudden death* is synonymous with cardiopulmonary arrest or heart–lung arrest. In the definition, the terms *sudden and unexpected* are extremely important. Cardiac arrest, when the heart stops pumping blood, may occur suddenly and unexpectedly for a number of reasons: heart attack; electric shock; asphyxiation; suffocation; drowning; allergic reaction; choking; or severe injury.

A person is considered clinically dead the moment the heart stops beating and breathing ceases. However, the vital centers of the central nervous system within the brain may remain viable for four to six minutes more. Resuscitation in the treatment of sudden death depends upon this grace period of four to six minutes. After that period, even though the heart might yet be restarted, the chance of return to a normal functional existence is lessened.

In sudden death, start CPR even if the four–to–six minute mark has been passed. However, the urgency of reestablishing the oxygenation system of the body, that is, ventilation and circulation, within the four–to–six minute grace period cannot be overemphasized.

Heart Attack

Diseases of the heart and blood vessels are the leading cause of death in the United States.

Recognition of the early warning signs is extremely important: uncomfortable pressure, squeezing, fullness, or dull pain in the center of the chest lasting for more than minutes; pain may radiate into the shoulders, arm, neck or jaw; sweating; nausea; shortness of breath; feeling of weakness; pale and sick looking.

A person need not exhibit all symptoms to have a heart attack. Symptoms may come and go, often leading the victim to attribute them to another cause such as indigestion.

Risk Factors

Certain factors have been identified as increasing an individual's risk of some form of cardiovascular disease. Some a person has no control over, such as sex, race, age and heredity; however, one can do a tremendous amount to improve physical condition and reduce the risk.

Recognizing the Problem

The person who initiates emergency heart–lung resuscitation has two responsibilities:

- ✓ To apply emergency measures to keep the clinically dead victim biologically alive

✓ To be sure the victim receives proper medical care

When sudden death occurs, the rescuer must act immediately to prevent biological death:

✓ Provide artificial ventilation to the lungs.

✓ Provide artificial circulation of the blood.

In addition to performing CPR, the rescuer must summon help to call an ambulance and/or a physician to the scene.

CPR Procedure for Single Rescuer

The CPR procedures should be learned and practiced on a training mannequin under the guidance of a qualified instructor. The step by step procedure is as follows:

- ✓ **Establish unresponsiveness.** Gently shake the victim's shoulder and shout, "Are you OK?" The response or lack of response will indicate if the victim is just sleeping or unconscious.
- ✓ **Call for help.** Help will be needed to assist in performing CPR or to call for medical help.
- ✓ **Position the victim.** If found in a crumpled up position and/or face down, the rescuer must roll the victim over; this is done while calling for help.

- ✓ When rolling the victim over, take care that broken bones are not further complicated by improper handling. Roll the victim as a unit so that the head, shoulders, and torso move simultaneously with no twisting.

- ✓ Kneel beside the victim, a few inches to the side.
- ✓ The victim's arm nearest the rescuer should be raised above the victim's head.
- ✓ The rescuer's hand closest to the victim's head should be placed on the victim's head and neck to prevent them from twisting.
- ✓ The rescuer should use the other hand to grasp under the victim's arm furthest from rescuer. This will be the point at which the rescuer exerts the pull in rolling the body over.
- ✓ Pull carefully under the arm, and the hips and torso will follow the shoulders with minimal twisting.
- ✓ Be sure to watch the neck and keep it in line with the rest of the body.
- ✓ The victim should now be flat on his or her back.

A–Airway. Open the airway. The most common cause of airway obstruction in an unconscious victim is the tongue.

- ✓ Use the head–tilt/chin–lift maneuver to open airway. (This maneuver is not recommended for a victim with possible neck or spinal injuries.)

B–Breathing. Establish breathlessness. After opening the airway establish breathlessness.

- ✓ Turn your head toward the victim's feet with your cheek close over the victim's mouth (3 to 5 seconds).
- ✓ **Look** for a rise and fall in the victim's chest.
- ✓ **Listen** for air exchange at the mouth and nose.
- ✓ **Feel** for the flow of air.

Sometimes opening and maintaining an open airway is all that is necessary to restore breathing.

- ✓ Provide artificial ventilation.
  - ✓ If the victim is not breathing give two full breaths by mouth–to–mouth, mouth–to–nose, or mouth–to–stoma ventilation.
  - ✓ Allow for lung deflation between each of the two ventilations.

C–Circulation. Check for pulse. Check the victim's pulse to determine whether external cardiac compressions are necessary.

- ✓ Maintain an open airway position by holding the forehead of the victim.
- ✓ Place your fingertips on the victim's windpipe and then slide them towards you until you reach the groove of the neck. Press gently on this area (carotid artery).

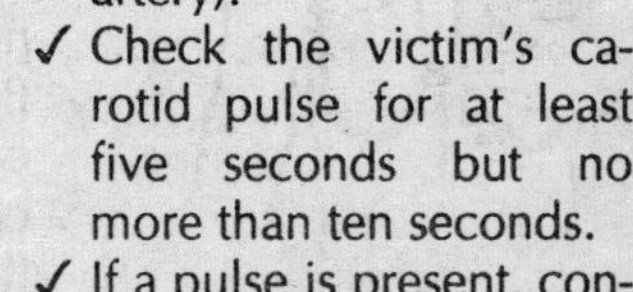

- ✓ Check the victim's carotid pulse for at least five seconds but no more than ten seconds.
- ✓ If a pulse is present, continue administering artificial ventilation once every five seconds or twelve times a minute. If not, make arrangements to send for trained medical assistance and begin CPR.
- ✓ **Perform cardiac compressions.**

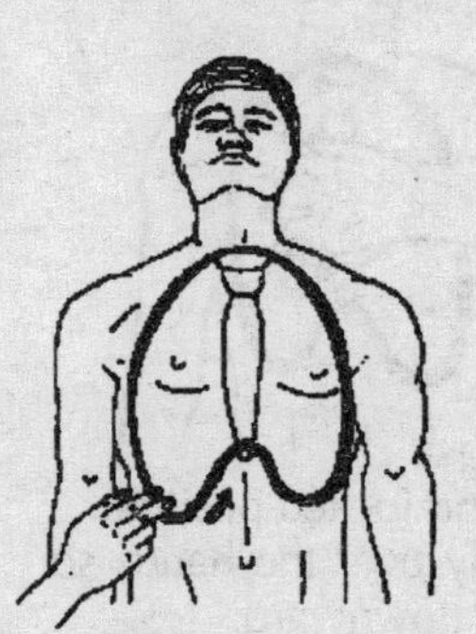

- ✓ Place the victim in a horizontal position on a hard, flat surface.
- ✓ Locate bottom of the rib cage with the index and middle fingers of your hand closest to patient's feet.

✓ Run your index finger up to or in the notch where the ribs meet the sternum (breastbone).

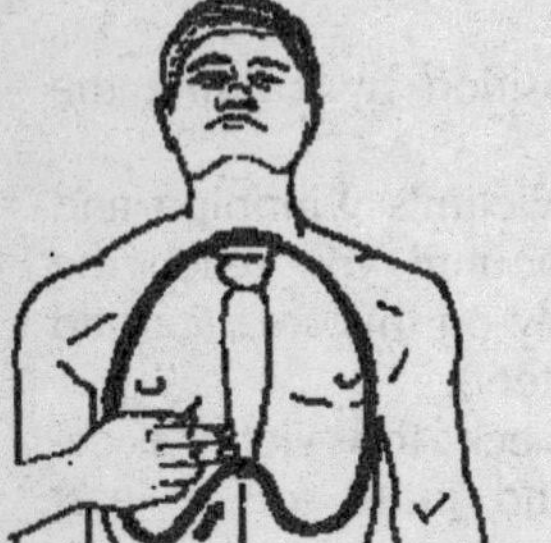

✓ Place your middle finger in notch and index finger on sternum.

✓ Place the heel of the other hand on the sternum next to the index finger in the notch in the rib cage.

✓ Place the hand used to locate the notch at the rib cage on top and parallel to the hand which is on the sternum.

✓ Keep the fingers off the chest, by either extending or interlocking them.

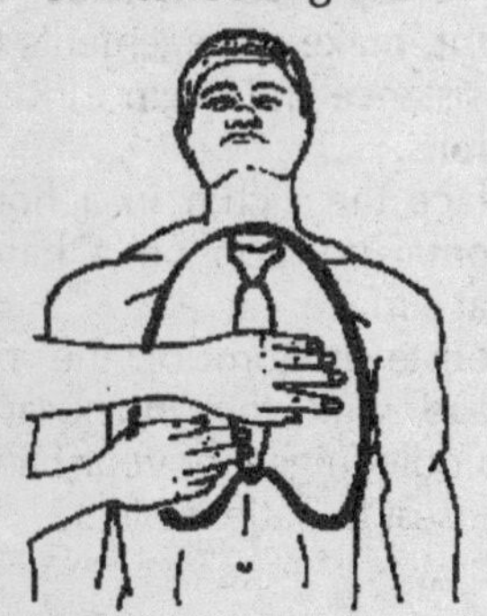

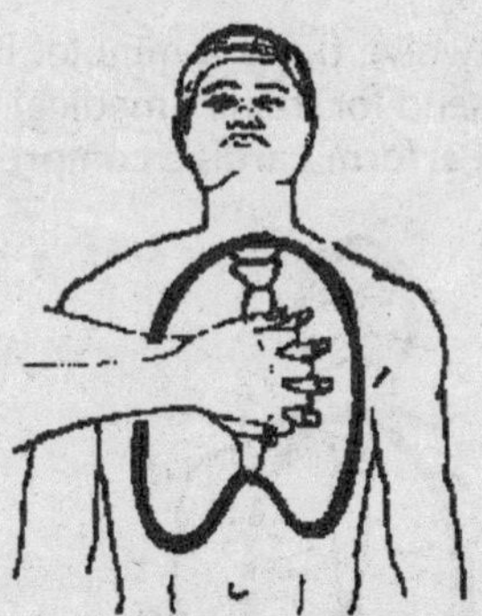

✓ Keep the elbows in a straight and locked position.

✓ Position your shoulders directly over the hands so that pressure is exerted straight downward.

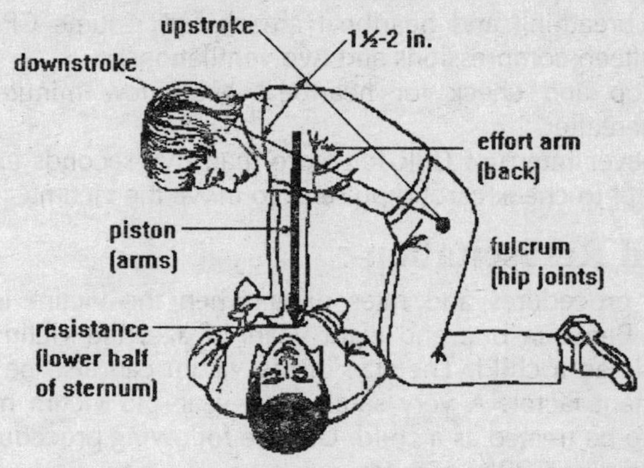

- ✓ Exert downward pressure to depress the sternum of an adult one and one–half to two inches.
- ✓ Each compression should squeeze the heart between the sternum and spine to pump blood through the body.
- ✓ Totally release pressure in order to allow the heart to refill completely with blood.
- ✓ Keep the heel of your hand in contact with the victim's chest at all times.
- ✓ Make compressions down and up in a smooth manner.

✓ Perform fifteen cardiac compressions at a rate of eighty to one hundred per minute, counting "one and, two and, three and," .... to fifteen.

✓ Use the head–tilt/chin–lift maneuver and give two full breaths (artificial ventilation).

✓ Repeat cycle four times (fifteen compressions and two ventilations).

✓ After the fourth cycle, recheck the carotid pulse in the neck for a heartbeat (five to ten seconds).

- ✓ If breathing and heartbeat are absent, resume CPR (fifteen compressions and two ventilations).
- ✓ Stop and check for heartbeat every few minutes thereafter.
- ✓ Never interrupt CPR for more than five seconds except to check carotid pulse or to move the victim.

Child Resuscitation

Some procedures and rates differ when the victim is a child. Between one and eight years of age, the victim is considered a child. The size of the victim can also be an important factor. A very small nine–year–old victim may have to be treated as a child. Use the following procedures when giving CPR to a child:

- ✓ Establish unresponsiveness by the shake and shout method.
- ✓ Open the airway using the head–tilt/chin–lift method.
- ✓ Establish breathlessness (three to five seconds).
- ✓ If the victim is not breathing, give two breaths.
- ✓ Check the carotid pulse for at least five seconds.
- ✓ Perform cardiac compressions.
  - ✓ Place the victim in a horizontal position on a hard, flat surface.
  - ✓ Use the index and middle fingers of your hand closest to the patient's feet to locate the bottom of the rib cage.
  - ✓ Place your middle finger in notch and index finger on sternum.
  - ✓ Heel of the other hand is placed on the sternum next to the index finger in the notch in the rib cage.
  - ✓ The fingers must be kept off the chest by extending them.
  - ✓ Elbow is kept straight by locking it.
  - ✓ The shoulders of the rescuer are brought directly

over the hand so that pressure is exerted straight downward.

- ✓ Exert enough pressure downward with one hand to depress the sternum of the child one to one and one–half inches.
- ✓ Compress at a rate of eighty to one hundred times per minute. Ventilate after every five compressions.

Infant Resuscitation

If the victim is younger than one year, it is considered an infant and the following procedures apply:

- ✓ Establish unresponsiveness by the shake and shout method.
- ✓ Open the airway; take care not to overextend the neck.
- ✓ Establish breathlessness (three to five seconds).
- ✓ Cover the infant's mouth and nose to get an airtight seal.
- ✓ Puff cheeks, using the air in the mouth to give two quick ventilations.
- ✓ Check the brachial pulse for five seconds.
- ✓ To locate the brachial pulse:
  - ✓ Place the tips of your index and middle fingers on the inner side of the upper arm.
  - ✓ Press slightly on the arm at groove in the muscle.
- ✓ If heartbeat is absent, begin CPR at once:
  - ✓ Place the index finger just under an imaginary line between the nipples on the infant's chest. Using the middle and ring fingers, compress chest one–half to one inch.
  - ✓ Compress at the rate of at least one hundred times per minute.
  - ✓ Ventilate after every five compressions.

Transporting the Victim

Do not interrupt CPR for more than five seconds unless absolutely necessary. However, when CPR is being performed and the victim must be moved for safety or transportation reasons, **do not** interrupt CPR for more than thirty seconds.

When moving a victim up or down a stairway, provide victim with effective CPR before interruption. Move the victim as quickly as possible and resume CPR at next level.

Termination of CPR

Under normal circumstances CPR may be terminated under one of four conditions:

- ✓ The victim is revived
- ✓ Another person trained in CPR relieves you
- ✓ The person performing CPR becomes exhausted and cannot continue
- ✓ A doctor pronounces the victim dead

Controlling Bleeding

Hemorrhaging or Bleeding

Hemorrhaging or bleeding is the escape of blood from an artery, vein, or capillary.

Bleeding from an Artery Arterial bleeding is characterized by bright red blood that spurts from a wound. Arterial blood comes direct from the heart; it is bright red from its fresh supply of oxygen and spurts at each contraction.

Bleeding from a Vein Dark red blood carrying waste that flows from a wound in a steady stream is from a vein.

Bleeding from Capillaries Blood from cut capillaries oozes and relatively little blood is lost. Usually direct pressure with a compress will cause the formation of a clot. When a large skin surface is involved, the threat of infection may be more serious than the loss of blood.

"Bleeders"

Some conditions, such as hemophilia or a side affect of medication do not allow normal clotting to occur. These persons may be in danger of bleeding to death even from slight wounds. This bleeding may be internal as well as external, and warrants close observation for shock. Apply compress bandages or gauze and rush the person to the nearest hospital for medical treatment.

Methods of Controlling Bleeding

External bleeding can usually be suppressed by applying direct pressure to the open wound. Direct pressure permits normal blood clotting to occur.

In cases of severe bleeding, the first aider may be upset by the appearance of the wound and the emotional state of the victim. Remember that a small amount of blood emerging from a wound spreads and appears as a lot of blood. It is important for the first aider to keep calm, keep the victim calm, and do what is necessary to relieve the situation. When it is necessary to control bleeding, use the following methods: direct pressure; elevation; pressure points; tourniquet (**as a last resort only**).

Direct Pressure

✓ The best method of controlling bleeding is to apply pressure directly to the wound by placing gauze or the cleanest material available against the bleeding point and applying firm pressure with the hand until a cover bandage can be applied. The cover bandage knot should be tied over the wound unless otherwise indicated. The bandage should not be removed until the victim is examined by a physician. Air splints or pressure bandages may be used over the heavy layer of gauze to supply direct pressure.

✓ Bleeding that continues after the bandage is in place indicates that not enough pressure has been applied. In such cases, **do not remove the original dressing**. Use the hand to put more pressure on the wound over the bandage, or apply a second bandage.

✓ In severe bleeding, if gauze or other suitable material is not available, the bare hand should be used to apply direct pressure immediately. This will control most bleeding.

Elevation

✓ Elevating the bleeding part of the body above the level of the heart will slow the flow of blood and speed clotting. Bleeding from a cut on the hand or arm will be slowed by raising the arm over the head. In the case of a foot wound, the victim should lie down with the leg propped up.

✓ Use elevation with direct pressure when there are no

fractures or fractures have been splinted and it will cause no pain or aggravation to the injury.

Pressure Points

Arterial bleeding can be controlled by applying pressure with the finger at *pressure points,* places over a bone where arteries are close to the skin. There are twenty–six pressure points on the body, thirteen on each side, situated along main arteries.

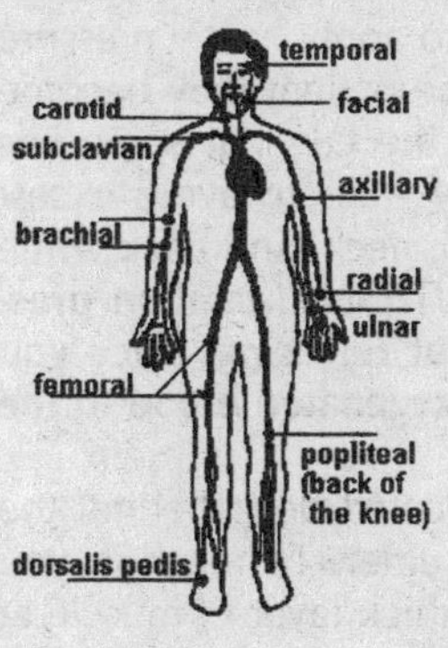

Use pressure points with caution, as indirect pressure may cause damage to the limb due to an inadequate flow of blood. When the use of a pressure point is necessary, **do not** substitute the indirect pressure for direct pressure on the wound; use both. Hold the pressure point only as long as necessary to stop the bleeding. Indirect pressure should be reapplied only if bleeding recurs.

The *temporal pressure point,* located slightly above and to the side of the eye, is used to control arterial bleeding from a scalp or head wound. It is important that this point be used for brief periods only as it can cut off blood to the brain and cause damage if held over thirty seconds.

The *facial pressure point* will help slow the flow of blood from a cut on the face. It should be used only for a minute or two. The pressure point is located in the "notch" along the lower edge of the bony structure of the jaw.

When there is bleeding from the neck, locate the trachea at the midline of the neck. Slide your fingers toward the site of the bleeding in the neck and feel for the pulsations of the carotid artery. Place your fingers over the artery, with your thumb behind the patient's neck. Apply pressure by squeezing your fingers toward your thumb. This action will compress the carotid artery against the trachea.

There are few occasions for using the *carotid pressure point*. **Do NOT use this method unless it is a part of your training.** If profuse bleeding from the neck is not controlled by direct pressure, you may have to use this technique. **NEVER apply pressure to both sides of the neck at the same time.** Take great care not to apply heavy pressure to the trachea. Stay alert because the patient may become faint or unconscious. Assume that the cervical spine has been injured and take all necessary steps to avoid excessive movement of the patient's head, neck, and back while you control profuse bleeding. **CAUTION: Maintain pressure for only a few seconds without releasing, since you are shutting off a large supply of oxygenated blood to the brain.**

The *subclavian pressure point* is located deep behind the collar bone in the "sink" of the shoulder. To reach it, you must push your thumb through the thick layer of muscle at the top of the shoulder and press the artery against the collar bone. It should be used only in extreme cases, such as amputation of the arm.

For wounds just above the elbow, the *axillary pressure point* is effective. Here, the artery just under the upper arm is pressed against the bone from underneath.

One of the most effective and most used pressure points for cuts on the lower arm is the *brachial point* at the elbow. Locate this pressure point in a groove on the inside of the arm and the elbow. To apply pressure, grasp the middle of the victim's arm with the thumb on the outside of the arm and the fingers on the inside. Press the fingers toward the thumb. Use the flat inside surface of the fingers, not the fingertips. This inward pressure closes the artery by pressing it against the arm bone.

The *radial pressure point* is located on the forearm close to the wrist on the thumb side of the hand and the *ulnar pressure point* is located on the little finger side of the wrist. The radial pressure point may be used for controlling bleeding at the wrist. Both pressure points must be used at the same time to control bleeding of the hand.

The *femoral artery* is often used to control severe bleeding from a wound on the lower extremity and the amputation of the leg. The pressure point is located on the front, center part of the crease in the groin area. This is where the artery crosses the pelvic basin on the way into the lower extremity. To apply pressure, position the victim flat on his or her back, if possible. Place the heel of one hand directly on the pressure point and apply the small amount of pressure needed to close the artery. If bleeding is not controlled, it may be necessary to press directly over the artery with the flat surface of the fingertips and apply additional pressure on the fingertips with the heel of the other hand.

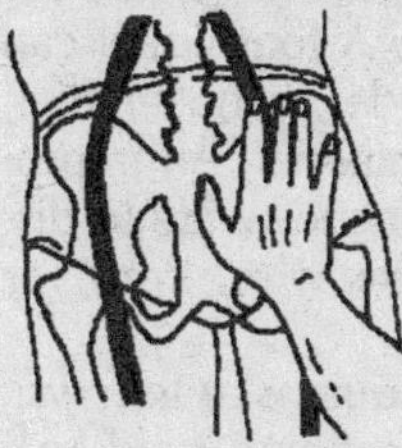

The *popliteal pressure point* at the back of the knee is the most effective point for controlling bleeding from a wound on the leg. The artery passes close to the surface of the skin, over the large bones in the knee joint.

The *dorsalis pedis pressure point* controls the bleeding in the lower foot and toes. It is found on the top of the foot.

Tourniquet

A tourniquet is used as an absolute last resort after all other methods have failed. First aiders should thoroughly understand the dangers and limitations of its use.

A tourniquet should be used only for life–threatening hemorrhage that cannot be controlled by other means. Improper use of a tourniquet by inexperienced, untrained persons may cause tissue injury or even death. The device itself often cuts into or injures the skin and underlying tissue. It is only required when large arteries are severed, in cases of partial or complete severance of a limb, and when bleeding is uncontrollable.

The standard tourniquet usually is a piece of web belting about thirty–six inches long, with a buckle or small device to hold it tightly in place when applied. A tourniquet can be improvised from a strap, belt, suspender, handkerchief, towel, necktie, cloth, or other suitable material. An improvised tourniquet should be at least two inches wide to distribute pressure over tissues. **NEVER use wire, cord, or anything that will cut into the flesh.**

The procedure for application of a tourniquet is as follows:

- ✓ While the proper pressure point is being held to temporarily control the bleeding, place the tourniquet between the heart and wound, with sufficient uninjured flesh between the wound and tourniquet.
- ✓ In using an improvised tourniquet, wrap the material tightly around the limb twice and tie in a half knot on the upper surface of the limb.
- ✓ Place a short stick or similar sturdy object at the half knot and tie a full knot.
- ✓ Twist the stick to tighten the tourniquet **only until the bleeding stops**.
- ✓ Secure the stick in place with the base ends of the tourniquet, another strip of cloth or suitable material.

Precautions:

- ✓ **Do not shield a tourniquet from view.**
- ✓ **Make a written note of the tourniquet's location and the time it was applied, and attach the note to the victim's clothing. Alternatively, make a "T" on the victim's forehead.**
- ✓ **Get the victim to a medical facility soon as possible.**

✓ **Once the tourniquet is tightened, it should not be loosened except by or on the advice of a doctor. The loosening of a tourniquet may dislodge clots and result in sufficient loss of blood to cause severe shock and death.**

Internal Bleeding

Internal bleeding in the chest or abdominal cavities usually results from a hard blow or fracture. Internal bleeding is usually not visible, but it can be very serious, even fatal. Internal bleeding may be determined by any or all of the following signs and symptoms:

- Pain, tenderness, swelling, or discoloration where injury is suspected
- Abdominal rigidity or muscle spasms
- Bleeding from mouth, rectum, or other natural body openings
- Showing symptoms of shock: dizziness, without other symptoms—dizziness when going from lying to standing may be the only early sign of internal bleeding; cold and clammy skin; eyes dull, vision clouded, and pupils enlarged; weak and rapid pulse; nausea and vomiting; shallow and rapid breathing; thirst; weak and helpless feeling

Emergency care for internal bleeding requires securing and maintaining an open airway, and treating for shock. **Never give the victim anything by mouth.**

Transport anyone suspected of having internal bleeding to professional medical help as quickly and safely as possible. Keep an injured person on his or her side when blood or vomit is coming from the mouth. Place the victim with chest injuries on the injured side if no spinal injuries are suspected. Transport the victim gently.

Nosebleeds

Nosebleeds are more often annoying than life threatening. They are more common during cold weather, when heated air dries out the nasal passages.

First aid for nosebleeds is simple:

- ✓ Keep the victim quietly seated, leaning forward if possible.
- ✓ Gently pinch the nostrils closed.
- ✓ Apply cold compresses to the victim's nose and face.
- ✓ If the person is conscious, it may be helpful to apply pressure beneath the nostril above the lip.
- ✓ Instruct victim not to blow his or her nose for several hours after bleeding has stopped or clots could be dislodged and start the bleeding again.

Nosebleeds that cannot be controlled through these measures may signal a more severe condition, such as high blood pressure. The victim should see a physician. Anyone who suffers a nosebleed after an injury should be examined for possible facial fractures.

If a fractured skull is suspected as the cause of a nosebleed, **do not** attempt to stop the bleeding. To do so might increase the pressure on the brain. Treat the victim for a fractured skull.

Shock

Medically, *shock* is the term used to describe the effects of inadequate circulation of the blood throughout the body. Shock may result from a variety of causes and can cause irreversible harm to the victim.

Nervous System

The nervous system plays an important role in shock. The various parts of the body and the organs controlling the body functions are coordinated by the two separate parts of the system: the voluntary and the involuntary.

The main parts of the nervous system consist of the brain, a collection of nerve centers, and the spinal cord. Nerves leaving the brain go into the spinal cord, pass down through the opening in the center of the spinal column, and branch off to all parts and organs of the body.

There are mainly two types of nerves entering and leaving the spinal cord: sensory nerves that convey sensations such as heat, cold, pain, and touch to the brain; and motor nerves that convey impulses from the brain to the muscles causing movement.

The involuntary system is a series of nerve centers in the chest and abdominal cavity along the spinal column. Each of these nerve centers controls vital organs and vital functions; through it involuntary muscles are stimulated to function without regard to our state of consciousness.

The cardiovascular system circulates blood to all cells, transporting nourishment and removing waste. The system is made up of blood vessels, blood, and the heart. The blood vessels dilate and constrict in response to signals transmitted to muscles in the blood vessel walls. Normally there is enough blood to fill the system—approximately ten to twelve pints for a person weighing 150 pounds.

Shock is the failure of this system to provide enough circulation of blood to every part of the body. Collapse of the cardiovascular system may be caused by any of three conditions: blood is lost; vessels dilate and there is insufficient blood to fill them; the heart fails to act properly as a pump and circulate the blood. No matter what the reason, the results are the same: an insufficient blood flow to provide adequate nourishment and oxygen to the body. Body process may slow down, reducing circulation and, without nourishment, organs begin to die, especially the brain.

Causes of Shock

The state of shock may develop rapidly or it may be delayed until hours after the event that triggers it. It occurs to some degree after every injury. It may be so slight as not to be noticed; or so serious that it results in death even when the injuries received ordinarily would not prove fatal.

Some of the major causes of shock are:

- Severe or extensive injuries
- Severe pain; loss of blood
- Severe burns
- Electrical shock
- Certain illnesses
- Allergic reactions
- Poisoning; exposure to extremes of heat and cold
- Emotional stress
- Substance abuse

The signs and symptoms of shock are both physical and emotional. Shock may be determined by any of the following conditions:

- Dazed look
- Paleness in light skinned individuals and ashen or grayish color in dark skinned individuals
- Nausea and vomiting
- Thirst

- Weak, rapid pulse
- Cold, clammy skin
- Shallow, irregular, labored breathing
- Pupils dilated
- Eyes dull and lackluster
- Cyanosis, or a bluish tinge to the skin (in the late stages of shock)

Some of the reactions bear directly on the symptoms presented. The most important reaction is a decided drop in blood flow, believed to be caused by the nervous system losing control over small blood vessels in the abdominal cavity. This is one of the reasons the victim is nauseous.

As blood fills the dilated vessels, decreased circulation near the surface causes the skin to become pale, cold, and clammy. Other areas suffer as well: the eyes are dull and lackluster and pupils may be dilated.

In the body's effort to fill the dilated blood vessels, less blood returns to the heart for recirculation. To overcome the decreased volume, the heart pumps faster but pumps a much lower quantity of blood per beat; therefore, the pulse is rapid and weak.

The brain suffers from this decreased blood supply and does not function normally; powers of reasoning, thinking, and expression are dulled. The victim may exhibit the following: weak and helpless feeling; anxiety; disorientation or confusion; unconsciousness (in the late stages of shock).

First Aid Treatment for shock

While life threatening, shock is reversible if recognized quickly and treated effectively. Maintain an open airway and ensure adequate breathing; control any bleeding.

First aid for the victim of physical shock is as follows:

- ✓ Keep the victim lying down, if possible. Make sure that the head is at least level with the body. Elevate the lower extremities if the injury will not be aggravated and there are no abdominal or head injuries. It may be necessary to raise the head and shoulders if a person is suffering from a head injury, sunstroke, heart attack, stroke, or shortness of breath due to a chest or throat injury. However, it should be noted that if an accident was severe enough to produce a head injury there may also be spinal damage. If in doubt, keep the victim flat.

✓ Provide the victim with plenty of fresh air.
✓ Loosen any tight clothing (neck, chest, and waist) in order to make breathing and circulation easier.
✓ Handle the victim as gently as possible and minimize movement.
✓ Keep the victim warm and dry by wrapping in blankets, clothing or other available material. These coverings should be placed under as well as over the victim to reduce the loss of body heat. Keep the victim warm enough to be comfortable. The objective is to maintain as near normal body temperature as possible—not to add heat.
✓ **Do not** give the victim anything by mouth.
✓ The victim's emotional well–being is just as important as his or her physical well–being. Keep calm and reassure the victim. Never talk to the victim about his or her injuries. Keep onlookers away from the victim as their conversation regarding the victim's injuries may be upsetting.

Anaphylactic Shock

Various technical terms describe different types of shock. At least one, anaphylactic shock, is a life–threatening emergency which requires rapid treatment.

Anaphylactic shock occurs when a person contacts something to which he or she is extremely allergic. People who are subject to anaphylactic shock should carry emergency medical identification at all times.

Substances that can cause anaphylactic shock may be in fish or shellfish, berries, or oral drugs such as penicillin. Insect stings (yellow jackets, wasps, hornets, etc.) or injected drugs can cause a violent reaction, as well as inhaled substances such as dust or pollen.

Sensitivity reactions can occur within a few seconds after contact. Death can result within minutes of contact; therefore, it is important that the first aider recognize the signs and symptoms of anaphylactic shock: itching or burning skin; hives covering a large area; swelling of the tongue and face; severe difficulty in breathing; tightening or pain in the chest; weak pulse; dizziness; convulsion; and coma.

Anaphylactic shock requires medication to counteract the allergic reaction. If the victim carries any medication to counteract the allergy, help the victim take the medicine.

Arrange for transportation to a medical facility as quickly as possible. Notify the hospital as to what caused the reaction. Maintain an open airway. If necessary, provide artificial ventilation and CPR and treat for physical shock.

Fainting

Fainting is a temporary loss of consciousness due to an inadequate supply of oxygen to the brain and is a mild form of shock. Fainting may be caused by the sight of blood, exhaustion, weakness, heat, or strong emotions such as fright, joy, etc. Some people faint more easily than others.
The signs and symptoms of fainting may be any or all of the following: the victim may feel weak and dizzy, and may see spots; the face becomes pale and the lips blue in both light and dark skinned people; the forehead is covered with cold perspiration; the pulse is rapid and weak; breathing is shallow.

The first aid for fainting is as follows:

- ✓ If the person feels faint, the initial response might be sitting with the head between the knees.
- ✓ Have the victim lie down with the head lower than the feet.
- ✓ If the victim is unconscious for any length of time, something may be seriously wrong. Arrange for transportation to a medical facility.
- ✓ Treat the victim for physical shock.
- ✓ Maintain an open airway.
- ✓ **Do not** give stimulants.

Treating Wounds

Open Wounds

An *open wound* refers to any break in the skin. Unbroken skin affords protection from most bacteria or germs; however, germs may enter through even a small break in the skin, and an infection may develop. Any open wound should receive prompt medical attention.

Breaks in the skin range from pin punctures or scratches to extensive cuts, tears, or gashes. An open wound may be the only surface evidence of a more serious injury such as a fracture, particularly in the case of head injuries involving fracture of the skull. In first aid, open wounds are divided into six classifications: abrasions, amputations, avulsions, incisions, lacerations, and punctures.

Abrasions Abrasions are caused by rubbing or scraping. These wounds are seldom deep, but a portion of the skin has been damaged, leaving a raw surface with minor bleeding. The bleeding in most abrasions is from the capillaries. Abrasions are easily infected due to the top layer of skin being removed, leaving the underlying skin exposed.

Amputations When an amputation occurs, the fingers, toes, hands, feet, or limbs are completely cut through or torn off which causes jagged skin and exposed bones. Bleeding may be excessive, or the force that amputates may close off torn vessels, limiting the amount of bleeding. A clean cut amputation seals off vessels and minimizes bleeding. A torn amputation usually bleeds heavily.

Avulsions An avulsion is an injury that tears an entire piece of skin and tissue loose or leaves it hanging as a flap. There is great danger of infection and bleeding. Body parts that have been wholly or partly torn off may sometimes be successfully reattached by a surgeon.

Incisions Wounds produced by a sharp cutting edge, such as a knife or razor. The edges of such wounds are smooth without bruising or tearing. If such a wound is deep, large blood vessels and nerves may be severed. Incised wounds bleed freely, and are often difficult to control.

Lacerations Lacerated wounds are those with rough or jagged edges. The flesh has been torn or mashed by blunt instruments, machinery, or rough edges such as a jagged piece of metal. Because the blood vessels are torn or mashed, these wounds may not bleed as freely as incised wounds. The ragged and torn tissues, with the foreign matter that is often forced or ground into the wound make it difficult to determine the extent of the damage. The danger of infection is great in lacerations.

Punctures Puncture wounds are produced by pointed objects such as needles, splinters, nails, or pieces of wire that pass through the skin and damage tissue in their path. The small number of blood vessels cut sometimes prevents free bleeding. The danger of infection in puncture wounds is great due to this poor drainage.

There are two types of puncture wounds: a *penetrating puncture wound* causes injured tissues and blood vessels whether it is shallow or deep; a *perforating puncture wound* passes through the body and out to create an exit wound which in many cases is more serious than the entrance wound.

First Aid for Open Wounds

The chief duties of a first aider in caring for open wounds are to stop bleeding and to prevent germs from entering the wound. If germs do not enter, there will be much less chance of infection and the wound will heal quickly.

- ✓ Carefully cut or tear the clothing so that the injury may be seen.
- ✓ If loose foreign particles are around the wound, wipe

them away with clean material. **Always wipe away from the wound, not toward it.**

✓ **Do not** attempt to remove an object impaled in the wound—serious bleeding and other damage may occur. Stabilize the object with a bulky dressing.

✓ **Do not** touch the wound with your hands, clothing, or anything that is not clean, if possible.

✓ Place a sterile bandage compress or gauze, when available, over the wound and tie in place.

✓ Dressings should be wide enough to completely cover the wound and the area around it.

✓ Protect compresses or gauze dressings with a cover bandage made from a cravat or triangular bandage. Place outer dressings on all open wounds except for wounds of the eye, nose, chin, finger and toe, or compound fractures of the hand and foot when splints are applied. Either use a cravat bandage or triangular bandage to cover the entire dressing.

✓ Unless otherwise specified, tie the knots of the bandage compress and outer dressing over the wound on top of the compress pad to help in checking the bleeding. However, when an open fracture is involved, tie away from wound.

✓ Keep victim quiet and lying still. Movement will increase circulation which could restart bleeding.

✓ Reassure the victim to ease emotional reaction.

✓ Treat for shock.

First Aid Dressings and Bandages

First aid materials for dressings and bandages include: bandage compress; gauze; roller bandage; adhesive compress; triangular bandage; cravat bandage.

Bandage Compress A special dressing intended to cover open wounds. It consists of a pad made of several thicknesses of gauze attached to the middle of a strip of gauze.

Pad sizes range from one to four inches. The strip of gauze at either side of the gauze pad is folded back so that it can be opened and the bandage compress tied in place with no disturbance of the sterile pad. The gauze of a bandage compress may be extended to twice its normal size by opening up folded gauze. Unless otherwise specified, all bandage compresses and all gauze dressings should be covered with an open triangular cravat or roller bandage.

BANDAGE COMPRESS

Gauze Gauze is used in several ways to apply first aid dressings. Plain gauze may be used in place of a bandage compress to cover large wounds and wounds of the trunk. In cases of profuse bleeding or where bulk is required to stabilize embedded objects, use several layers of gauze. Care should be taken not to touch the portion of the gauze that is to be placed in contact with the wound.

Gauze Roller Bandage The gauze roller bandage is a self-adhering form-fitting bandage. It can be made secure with several snug overlapping wraps, then tied in place.

Adhesive Compress An adhesive compress is a self-adhering bandage that has gauze to cover the wound and a sticky backing which holds to the victim's skin.

Triangular Bandage A standard triangular bandage is made from a piece of cloth approximately forty inches square by folding the square diagonally and cutting along the fold. It is easily applied and can be handled so that the part to be applied over a wound will not be soiled. A triangular bandage does not tend to slip off once it is correctly applied.

The bandage is usually made from unbleached cotton cloth, although any kind of cloth will do. In emergencies, a triangular bandage can be improvised from a clean handkerchief, a clean piece of shirt, etc.

OPEN TRIANGULAR BANDAGE

The triangular bandage is also used to make improvised tourniquets, to support fractures and dislocations, to apply splints, and to form slings. If a regular–size bandage is found to be too short when a dressing is applied, it can be lengthened by tying another bandage to one end.

Cravat Bandage A triangular bandage may be used open or folded. When folded, it is known as a cravat. A cravat bandage is prepared as follows:

- ✓ Make a one inch fold along the base of the triangular bandage.
- ✓ Bring the point to the center of the folded base, placing the point underneath the fold, to make a *wide cravat* bandage.

WIDE CRAVAT BANDAGE

- ✓ A *medium cravat* is made by folding lengthwise along a line midway between the base and the new top of the bandage, in effect, folding the wide cravat bandage in half lengthwise.
- ✓ A *narrow cravat* is made by repeating the folding.

This method has the advantage that all bandages can be folded to a uniform width, or the width may be varied to suit the purpose for which it is to be used. To complete a dressing, the ends of the bandage are tied securely.

Square Knot

Unless otherwise specified, all knots or ties mentioned should be tied in a square knot.

To tie a square knot, take an end of the bandage in each hand, pass the end in the right hand over and around the end in the left and tie a single knot. Then pass the end now in the left hand over the end in the right hand, and complete the knot. Each loose end, after the second knot is tied, will be doubled back and lying against itself with the other end wrapped around it. The rule to remember in tying a square knot is right over left, then left over right.

This knot can be untied easily by converting it into a slip knot. Grasp one tail of the bandage in one hand, hold the bandage with the other hand, and pull the tail under the knot rolls. Release the tail, and with the free hand grasp the knot, holding it firmly; with the other hand, pull the bandage away from the knot.

Slings

Slings are used to support injuries of the shoulder, upper extremities or ribs. In an emergency they may be improvised from belts, neckties, scarves, or similar articles. Bandages should be used if available.

Triangular Bandage Sling

Tie a triangular bandage sling as follows:

- ✓ Place one end of the base of an open triangular bandage over the shoulder on the injured side.
- ✓ Allow the bandage to hang down in front of the chest so that the apex, or point, will be behind the elbow of the injured arm.
- ✓ Bend the arm at the elbow with hand slightly elevated (four to five inches).
- ✓ Bring forearm across the chest and over the bandage.
- ✓ Carry the lower end of the bandage over the shoulder on the uninjured side and tie at uninjured side of the neck, being sure the knot is at the side of the neck.

✓ Twist the apex of the bandage, and tuck it in at the elbow.

The hand should be supported with the fingertips exposed, whenever possible, to permit detection of interference with circulation.

Cravat Bandage Sling

Tie a cravat bandage sling as follows:

✓ Place one end over the shoulder on the injured side.
✓ Allow the bandage to hang down in front of the chest.
✓ Bend the arm at the elbow with hand slightly elevated four to five inches.
✓ Bring the forearm across the chest and over the bandage.
✓ Carry the lower end of the bandage over the injured arm to the shoulder on the uninjured side and tie at uninjured side of neck.

Basket Sling

A useful sling for transporting or handling a victim with a suspected neck injury or an unconscious victim whose arms may create difficulties, can be made with an open triangular bandage as follows:

✓ Place an open triangular bandage across the chest with the apex down.
✓ Fold the arms over one another on the bandage. Bring the ends of the base together and tie.
✓ Cross the apex over the folded arms and tie to the knotted ends of the base.

Principles of Bandaging

✓ Bandage wounds snugly, but not too tight. Too tight a bandage may damage surrounding tissue or interfere with blood supply, especially if swelling occurs. A bandage tied too loosely may slip off the wound.

- ✓ In bandaging the arms or the legs, leave the tips of the fingers or toes uncovered where possible to detect any interference with circulation.
- ✓ If the victim complains that the bandage is too tight, loosen it and make it comfortable, but snug. Unless otherwise specified, all knots should be tied over open wounds to help control bleeding.
- ✓ If bandages become saturated with blood, apply additional bandages or dressings. **Do not** remove original dressing.

Dressings for Wounds

The following dressings are recommended for covering wounds.

Scalp, Temple, Ear, or Face

To dress an open wound for the scalp, temple, ear, or face, proceed as follows:

- ✓ Apply the pad of a bandage compress over the wound.
- ✓ Carry one end under the chin, and the other over the top of the head.
- ✓ Cross at the temple in front of the ear on the side opposite the injury.
- ✓ Bring one end around the front of the head and the other end low around the back of the head.
- ✓ Tie on or near the compress pad.

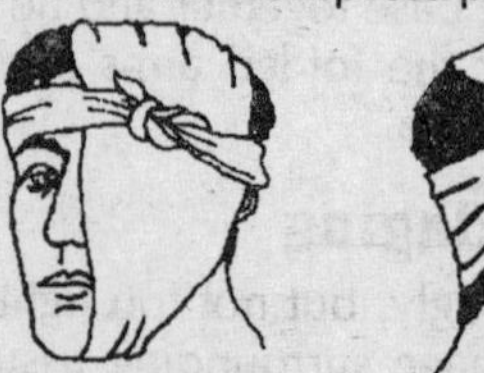

- ✓ Cover the compress with a cravat bandage applied in the same manner.

If the wound is on the cheek or the front of the face, cross the bandage compress and cravat bandage behind the ear, on the side opposite the injury; bring the ends around the forehead and back of the head, and tie.

Extensive Wounds of the Scalp

A wound or wounds involving a large area of the scalp may be dressed by covering the injury with a piece of gauze or a large bandage compress.

- ✓ Apply the pad of a sterile compress to the wound.
- ✓ Carry one end under the chin and the other end over the top of the head.
- ✓ Cross the ends at the temple.
- ✓ Carry one end around the forehead.
- ✓ Pass the other end around the back of the head and tie on the opposite side of the face.
- ✓ Next apply a triangular bandage over the head with the base snugly across the forehead, just above the eyebrows and the apex of the bandage at the back of the neck.
- ✓ Bring the two ends of the bandage around the head just above the ears.
- ✓ Cross under the bony prominence on the back of the head.
- ✓ Return the ends to the middle of the forehead.
- ✓ Tie just above the eyebrows.
- ✓ Fold up the apex and tuck it in snugly over the crossed ends at the back of the head.

When gauze is used, take care to keep it in place while the cover bandage is being applied.

Forehead or Back of Head

To dress an open wound of the forehead or back of the head, proceed as follows:

- ✓ Apply the pad of a sterile bandage compress over the injury.
- ✓ Hold the compress in place by passing the ends of the compress around the head above the ears, and tying over the compress pad.
- ✓ Apply the center of a cravat bandage over the pad, take the ends around the head, cross them, and tie over the compress pad.

Eye Injuries

Objects embedded in the eye should be removed only by a doctor. Such objects must be protected from accidental movement or removal until the victim receives medical attention.

- ✓ Tell the victim that both eyes must be bandaged to protect the injured eye.
- ✓ Encircle the eye with a gauze dressing or other suitable material.
- ✓ Position a cup or cone over the embedded object. The object should not touch the top or sides of the cup. It may be necessary to make a hole in the bottom of the cup if the object is longer than the cup.

- ✓ Hold the cup and dressing in place with a bandage compress or roller bandage that covers both eyes. It is important to bandage both eyes to prevent movement of the injured eye.
- ✓ Never leave the victim alone, as the victim may panic with both eyes covered. Keep in hand contact so the victim will always know someone is there.

- ✓ Stabilize the head with sand bags or large pads and always transport the victim on his or her back.
- ✓ Ensure that the victim does not tamper with the dressing or embedded object.

This procedure should also be used for lacerations and other injuries to the eyeball.

After a serious injury, the eyeball may be knocked out of the socket. No attempt should be made to put the eye back into the socket. The eye should be covered with a moist dressing and a protective cup without applying pressure to the eye. A bandage compress or roller bandage that covers both eyes should be applied. Transport the victim face up with the head immobilized.

For all injuries to and around the upper or lower lid of the eye, use a sterile bandage compress as follows:

- ✓ Place the center of a bandage compress over the injured eye.
- ✓ Carry the end on the injured side below the ear to the back of the head.
- ✓ Carry the other end above the ear on the opposite side.
- ✓ Tie toward the injured side below the bony prominence on the back of the head.
- ✓ Bring both ends over the top of the head, passing the longer end under the dressing at the temple on the uninjured side.
- ✓ Slide it in front of the uninjured eye and pull it tightly enough to raise the dressing above the uninjured eye.
- ✓ Tie to the other end on top of the head.

Nose

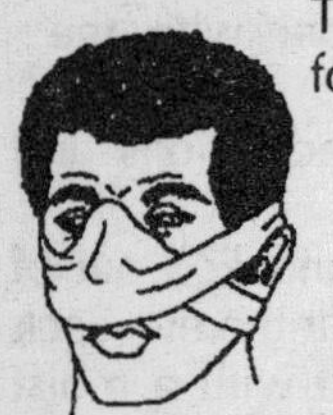

To bandage a wound to the nose, proceed as follows:

- ✓ Split the tails of a bandage compress.
- ✓ Apply the pad of the compress to the wound.
- ✓ Pass the top tails, one to each side of the head below the ears and tie at the back of the neck.
- ✓ Pass the bottom tails, one to each side of the head above the ears and tie at the back of the head.

Chin

In order to tie a bandage for a wound on the chin, proceed as follows:

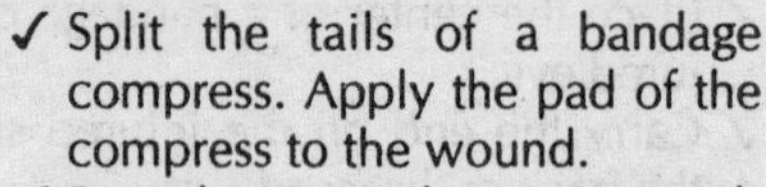

- ✓ Split the tails of a bandage compress. Apply the pad of the compress to the wound.
- ✓ Pass the top tails, one to each side of the neck, below the ears and tie at the back of the neck.
- ✓ Pass the bottom tails, one to each side of the head in front of the ears and tie at the top of the head.

Neck or Throat

To bandage a wound on the neck or throat, proceed as follows:

- ✓ Apply the pad of a sterile bandage compress to the wound.
- ✓ Pass the ends around the neck, and tie over the wound.
- ✓ Place the center of cravat bandage over the compress.
- ✓ Pass the ends of the cravat bandage around the neck,

cross them, bring them around the neck again, and tie loosely.

- ✓ Use hand pressure over the wound for control of excessive bleeding.

Shoulder

In order to tie a bandage for a wound of the shoulder, proceed as follows:

- ✓ Apply the pad of a bandage compress over the wound. Bring the ends under the armpit.
- ✓ Cross, carry to the top of the compress, cross, carry one end across the chest and one end across the back, and tie in the opposite armpit over a pad.
- ✓ Place the apex of a triangular bandage high up on the shoulder. Place the base, along which a hem has been folded, below the shoulder on the upper part of the arm, carry the ends around the arm and tie them on the outside.
- ✓ To hold the bandage in position, place the center of a cravat bandage under the opposite armpit; carry the ends to the shoulder over the apex of the first bandage; tie a single knot; then fold the apex over and complete the knot.
- ✓ Place the forearm in a triangular bandage sling.

Armpit

To dress a wound of the armpit, proceed as follows:

- ✓ Apply the pad of a bandage compress over the wound. Lift the arm only high enough to apply compress, as further damage may occur to lacerated nerves which are close to the surface.
- ✓ Carry the ends over the shoulder and cross.
- ✓ Carry one end across the chest and the other end across the back.
- ✓ Tie under the opposite arm over a pad.

> **If there is severe bleeding**, place a hard object

over the pad of the compress and push it well up into the armpit, holding the pads in place by a cravat bandage.

- ✓ Place the center of a cravat bandage over the wound.
- ✓ Bring the ends over the shoulder, crossing them; then pass the ends around the chest and back and tie them under the opposite arm. Next bring the arm down and secure it firmly against the chest wall by a cravat bandage passed around the arm and chest. Tie securely on the opposite side over a pad.
- ✓ Place the forearm in a triangular sling.

Arm, Forearm, and Wrist

To bandage wounds of the arm, forearm, and wrist, proceed as follows:

- ✓ Apply the pad of a sterile bandage compress over the wound.
- ✓ Pass the ends several times around the arm and tie them over the pad.
- ✓ Place the center of a cravat bandage over the pad.
- ✓ Pass the ends around the arm, cross them, continue around the arm and tie over the pad.
- ✓ Place the forearm and hand in a triangular sling.

Elbow

To dress a wound of the elbow, proceed as follows:

- ✓ Start with joint in a slightly bent position.
- ✓ Apply the pad of a bandage compress over the wound.
- ✓ Pass the ends of the bandage around the elbow and carry them around the arm just above the elbow.
- ✓ Cross them and carry them around the forearm just below the elbow.
- ✓ Tie at a point below the elbow.

Cover with a cravat bandage as follows:

- ✓ Place the center of the cravat bandage over the point

of the elbow.

- ✓ Pass the ends around and cross them above the point of the elbow.
- ✓ Carry them around the arm and cross again at the bend of the elbow.
- ✓ Carry around the forearm, and tie just below the point of the elbow.
- ✓ Immobilize the upper extremity by placing the forearm in a triangular sling.

Palm or Back of Hand

To dress a wound of the palm or back of the hand, proceed as follows:

- ✓ Apply the pad of a bandage compress over the wound.
- ✓ Pass the ends several times around the hand and wrist.
- ✓ Tie over the pad.

- ✓ Place the center of a cravat bandage over the pad.
- ✓ Cross the ends at the opposite side of the hand.
- ✓ Pass one end around the little finger side of the hand.
- ✓ Pass the other end between the thumb and forefinger, taking the ends to the wrist.
- ✓ Cross the ends and continue around the wrist, crossing at the back of the wrist.
- ✓ Cross again at the inside of the wrist.
- ✓ Tie at the back of the wrist.
- ✓ Place forearm and hand in triangular bandage sling.

Extensive Wounds of the Hand

Control arterial bleeding of the hand.

To dress extensive wounds of the hand, proceed as follows:

- ✓ Apply gauze or a bandage compress over the wound.
- ✓ When there are multiple wounds of fingers, separate the fingers with gauze.
- ✓ If a bandage compress is used, pass the ends several times around the hand and wrist.
- ✓ Tie them over the pad.

Cover the hand with a triangular bandage as follows:

- ✓ Place the base on the inner side of the wrist.
- ✓ Bring the apex down over the back of the hand.

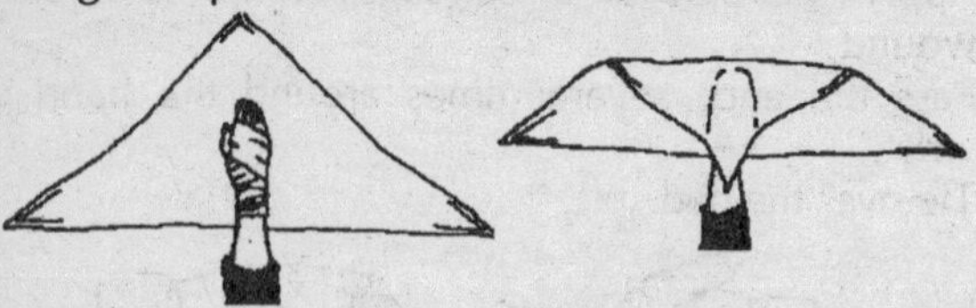

- ✓ Cross the ends (little finger side first) over the back of the hand and wrist.

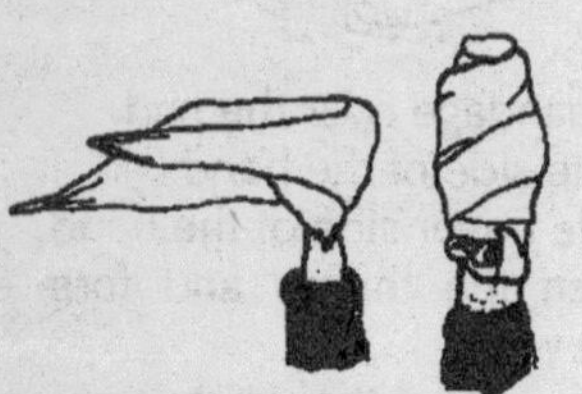

- ✓ Wrap around wrist, ending in tie on the back of the wrist.
- ✓ Bring the apex down over the knot and tuck it under.
- ✓ Place the forearm and hand in a triangular bandage sling.
- ✓ If there is swelling, elevate and apply ice.

Finger

To dress a wound of the finger, proceed as follows:

- ✓ Apply the pad of a small bandage compress over the wound.

✓ Pass the ends several times around the finger and tie over the pad.
✓ A small adhesive compress may be used instead of a bandage compress for a wound of the finger or a wound on the end of the finger. A bent finger should be dressed bent and not fully extended.
✓ If more than one finger is injured, cover with an open triangular bandage as for extensive wounds of the hand.

Chest or Back Between Shoulder Blades

To dress a wound on the chest or back between the shoulder blades, proceed as follows:

✓ Place the pad of the compress over the wound so that the ends are diagonally across the chest or back.
✓ Carry one end over the shoulder and under the armpit. Carry the other end under the armpit and over the shoulder. Tie the ends over the compress.

Cover the compress and chest or back with a triangular bandage as follows:

✓ Place the center of the base at the lower part of the neck.
✓ Allow the apex to drop down over the chest or back, as appropriate.
✓ Carry the ends over the shoulders and under the armpits to the center of the chest or back.
✓ Tie with the apex below the knot.
✓ Turn the apex up and tuck it over the knot.

Back, Chest, Abdomen, Or Side

To tie a bandage for the back, chest, abdomen, or side, proceed as follows:

✓ Apply the pad of a sterile bandage compress or sterile gauze over the wound. If a sterile bandage compress is used, take the ends around the body (one end across the back and the other across the abdomen or chest and tie on the side).

- ✓ Cover with a proper size cravat bandage by placing the center of the bandage on the side nearest the injury.
- ✓ Take the ends across the back and abdomen or chest and tie on the opposite side.

NOTE: If air is being sucked into the lungs through a wound in the chest, cover the wound immediately with a nonporous material, such as plastic wrap, wax paper, or your hand; then dress the wound. Transport the victim to a medical facility as quickly as possible.

Protruding Intestines

To dress a wound in which the victim's intestines are protruding, proceed as follows:

- ✓ Place the victim on his or her back with something under the knees to raise them and help relax the abdominal muscles.
- ✓ **Do not** try to re–place the intestines; leave the organ on the surface.
- ✓ Cover with aluminum foil, plastic wrap, or a moist dressing.
- ✓ Cover lightly with an outer dressing. This will help preserve heat.

Lower Abdomen, Back, or Buttocks

To dress a wound of the lower part of the abdomen, the lower part of the back or the buttocks, proceed as follows:

- ✓ Apply a pad made from several layers of sterile gauze; in the absence of gauze, the pad of a sterile compress may be placed over the wound and held in place by passing the ends around the body and tying them.
- ✓ Cover the gauze or bandage compress with two triangular bandages:
    - ✓ Tie the apexes in the crotch.

- ✓ Bring the base of one bandage up on the abdomen.
- ✓ Pass the ends around to the back and tie.
- ✓ Pass the ends of the other bandage around to the front and tie.

Groin

To dress a wound of the groin, proceed as follows:

- ✓ Apply the pad of a bandage compress over the wound.
- ✓ Carry the ends to the hip and cross.
- ✓ Carry the ends across to the opposite side of the body and tie.

Cover the compress with two cravat bandages tied together as follows:

- ✓ Place the center of one of the cravat bandages over the pad and follow the compress in such a manner as to cover it entirely.
- ✓ Continue with the other cravat bandage around the entire body a second time and tie.

Crotch

To bandage a wound of the crotch, proceed as follows:

- ✓ Cover wound with sterile gauze.
- ✓ Pass a narrow cravat bandage around the waist and tie in front, leaving the ends to hang free.
- ✓ Pass a second cravat bandage under the knot of the first cravat bandage.
- ✓ Pass the two ends of the second cravat bandage between the thighs and bring one end around each hip.
- ✓ Tie to the ends of the cravat bandage tied around the body.

Hip

To dress a wound of the hip, proceed as follows:

- ✓ Split the tails of a bandage compress.
- ✓ Place the pad over the wound.
- ✓ Pass the top tails around the body.
- ✓ Tie over the opposite hip.
- ✓ Pass the ends of the bottom tails around thigh and cross on inside of thigh.
- ✓ Continue around the thigh, tying on the outside.

Cover with a triangular bandage as follows:

- ✓ Place the base of a triangular bandage on the thigh with the apex pointing up; bring the ends of the base around the thigh, and tie.
- ✓ Pass a second cravat bandage around the body at the waist and tie a single knot over the apex of the triangular bandage.
- ✓ Fold the apex over the knot and complete tying the knot.

Thigh or Leg

To tie a bandage for a wound of the thigh or leg, proceed as follows:

- ✓ Apply the pad of a bandage compress over the wound.
- ✓ Pass the ends around the injured extremity and tie over the pad.
- ✓ Place the center of a cravat bandage over the compress, pass the ends around the injured part, cross them, bring them around again, and tie over the pad.

Knee

To dress a wound of the knee, proceed as follows:

- ✓ Apply the pad of a sterile bandage compress over the wound.
- ✓ Cross the ends at the back of the knee and return to

the front of the knee.

- ✓ Tie firmly over the pad, if possible.
- ✓ Place the center of a cravat bandage over the pad.
- ✓ Bring the ends of the bandage around each side of the leg.
- ✓ Cross them at the back of the knee, pull them forward, and tie them above the knee.

Ankle

To dress a wound of the ankle, proceed as follows:

- ✓ Apply the pad of a bandage compress to the wound.
- ✓ Carry the ends to the top of the instep and cross.
- ✓ Carry the ends around the bottom of the foot and cross over the instep again.
- ✓ Pass the ends around the ankle and tie over the pad.
- ✓ Place the center of a cravat bandage over the compress.
- ✓ Carry the ends to the top of the instep, cross.
- ✓ Cross the ends under the foot, bring back to the top of the instep and cross.
- ✓ Carry the ends around the ankle and tie over the pad.

Foot

To dress a wound of the foot proceed as follows:

- ✓ Apply the pad of a bandage compress to the wound.
- ✓ Carry the ends around the foot and ankle.
- ✓ Tie over the pad.
- ✓ Place center of a cravat bandage over the compress.
- ✓ Carry the ends around the foot and ankle, ending in a tie as near the front of the ankle as possible.

Extensive Wounds of Foot or Toes

First, control arterial bleeding of the foot.

To dress extensive wounds of the foot and toes, proceed as follows:

- ✓ Apply gauze or the pad of a large bandage compress over the wound and tie it in place.
- ✓ Place the base of a triangular bandage on the back of the ankle.
- ✓ Bring the apex under the sole of the foot, over the toes, back over the instep, and up the leg to a point above the ankle in front.
- ✓ Pass the end on the little toe side over the instep, then the other end over the instep, and continue around the ankle with both ends and tie in front.
- ✓ Bring the apex down over the knot and tuck in under the knot.

Toe

To dress a wound of the toe, proceed as follows:

- ✓ Apply the pad of a small bandage compress over the wound.
- ✓ Pass the ends around the toe several times and tie over the pad.
- ✓ Instead of a bandage compress a small adhesive compress may be used for a wound of the toe or a wound on the end of the toe.
- ✓ When there are multiple wounds of the toes, separate the toes with gauze. Cover with a triangular bandage as described for extensive wounds of the foot.

Closed Wounds

Closed wounds are injuries where the skin is not broken, but damage occurs to underlying tissues. These injuries may result in internal bleeding from damage to internal organs, muscles, and other tissues. Closed wounds are classified as: bruises; or ruptures or hernias.

Bruises

Bruises are caused by an object striking the body or the body coming into contact with a hard object. The skin is not broken, but the soft tissue beneath the skin is damaged. Small blood vessels are ruptured, causing blood to seep into surrounding tissues, producing swelling. The injured area appears red at first, then darkens to blue or purple. When large blood vessels have been ruptured or large amounts of underlying tissue have been damaged, a lump called a hematoma or blood tumor may develop as a result of blood collecting within the damaged tissue.

The symptoms of a bruise are: immediate pain; swelling; rapid discoloration; later, pain or pressure on movement.

The first aid for bruises is as follows:

- ✓ To limit swelling and reduce pain, apply an ice bag, a cloth wrung out in cold water, or a chemical cold pack.
- ✓ Elevate the injured area and place at complete rest.
- ✓ Check for fractures and other possible injuries.
- ✓ Treat for shock.

Severe bruises should have the care of a doctor.

Ruptures or Hernias

The most common rupture or hernia is a protrusion of a portion of an internal organ through the wall of the abdomen. Most ruptures occur in or just above the groin, but may occur at other places. Ruptures result from a combination of weakness of the tissues and muscular strain.

The symptoms of a rupture are: sharp, stinging pain; feeling of something giving away at the site of the rupture; swelling; possible nausea and vomiting.

First aid for a rupture is as follows:

- ✓ Place the victim on his or her back with the knees well drawn up.
- ✓ Place a blanket or similar padding under the knees.
- ✓ Place the center of a cravat under the padding, bring the ends above the knees and tie.
- ✓ Place the center of two cravat bandages tied together at the ends on the outside of the thighs and pass the ends around the thighs, cross under the blanket, bring the ends around the legs just above the ankles and tie.
- ✓ Never attempt to force the protrusion back into the cavity.
- ✓ Place cold application to the injured area.
- ✓ Cover with a blanket.
- ✓ The victim should be transported lying down with the knees drawn up.

Foreign Bodies

Foreign Bodies in the Eye

Particles of dirt, dust, or fine pieces of metal may enter the eye and lodge there. If not removed, they can cause discomfort, inflammation and possibly, infection.

Through an increased flow of tears, nature limits the possibility of harm by dislodging many of these substances. **Do not** let the victim rub the eye. Rubbing may scratch the delicate eye tissues or force sharp objects into the tissues. The first aider should not attempt to remove foreign bodies. It is always safer to send the person to a physician.

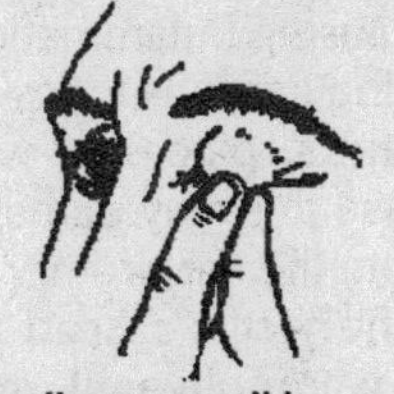
pull upper eyelid over lower eyelashes

lift eyelid, remove object with sterile gauze

To remove a foreign body on the inside of the eyelid:

- ✓ Pull upper eyelid down over the lower eyelashes.
- ✓ Lift eyelid and remove object with sterile gauze.

The first aid for a foreign body on the eye that is not on the cornea or imbedded is as follows:

- ✓ Flush the eye with clean water, if available, for 15 minutes. If necessary, hold the eyelids apart.
- ✓ Often a foreign body lodged under the upper eyelid can be removed by drawing the upper lid down over the lower lid; as the upper lid is drawn over the lashes of the lower lid, the foreign body is removed by the wiping action of the eyelashes.
- ✓ A foreign body on the surface of the eye may also be removed by grasping the eyelashes of the upper lid and turning the lid over a cotton swab or similar object. The particle is then carefully removed with the corner of a piece of sterile gauze.

If a foreign body becomes lodged in the eyeball, **do not** attempt to disturb it, as it may be forced deeper into the eye and result in further damage. Place a compress over both eyes. Keep the victim calm and get medical help.

Foreign Bodies in the Ear

Small insects, pieces of rock, or other material may become lodged in the ear. Children sometimes put objects, such as kernels of corn, peas, buttons or seeds in their ears. Such objects as seeds absorb moisture and swell, making their removal difficult and often causing inflammation. The first aid for foreign bodies in the ear is as follows:

- ✓ **Do not** insert pins, match sticks, pieces of wire or other objects in the ear because this may damage the tissue lining the ear or perforate the ear drum.
- ✓ In the case of insects, turn the victim's head to the side and put several drops of warm olive oil, mineral oil, or baby oil in the ear; then let the oil run out and the drowned insect may come out with it. **Do not** try to flush out objects with water.
- ✓ Consult a physician if a foreign body cannot be easily removed.

Foreign Bodies in the Nose

Foreign bodies in the nose usually can be removed easily, but occasionally the services of a physician are required. The first aid for a foreign body in the nose is as follows:

- ✓ Induce sneezing by sniffing snuff or pepper, or tickling the opposite nostril with a feather. This will usually dislodge a foreign body in the nose.
- ✓ **Do not** blow the nose violently or with one nostril held shut.
- ✓ **Do not** attempt to dislodge the foreign body with a hairpin or similar object. This method may damage tissues of the nasal cavity or push the foreign body into an inaccessible place.

Foreign Bodies in the Stomach

Foreign bodies such as pins coins, nails, and other objects are sometimes swallowed accidentally. Except for pins, nails, or other sharp objects, foreign objects that are swallowed usually cause no great harm.

- ✓ **Do not** induce vomiting or bowel movement.
- ✓ Consult a physician immediately.

Burns and Scalds

Classification of Burns

Burns may be classified according to extent and depth of damage as follows:

- **First degree (Minor)** Burned area is painful. Outer skin is reddened. Slight swelling is present.
- **Second degree (Moderate)** Burned area is painful. Underskin is affected. Blisters may form. The area may have a wet, shiny appearance because of exposed tissue.
- **Third degree (Critical)** Insensitive due to the destruction of nerve endings. Skin is destroyed. Muscle tissues and bone underneath may be damaged. The area may be charred, white, or grayish in color.

Burns may also be classified according to cause. The four major types of burns by cause are: chemical; thermal; electrical; and radiation.

The seriousness of a burn or scald is influenced by the extent of the body surface involved, as well as by the depth to which the tissue has been penetrated. It is generally assumed that where two–thirds of the surface of the body is injured by a second degree burn or scald, death will usually follow, but a much smaller area injured by a third–degree burn can also cause death.

Burns can damage muscles, bones, nerves, and blood vessels. The eyes can be burned beyond repair. The respiratory system structures can be damaged, with possible airway obstruction, respiratory failure, and respiratory arrest. In addition to the physical damage caused by burns, victims also may suffer emotional and psychological problems that could last a lifetime.

Shock is very severe when burns are extensive and may cause death in a few hours.

First Aid for Burns

The first aid given to a burn victim largely depends on the cause of the burn and the degree of severity.

Emergency first aid for burns or scalds should primarily be:

- ✓ Exclusion of air from the burned area
- ✓ Relief of the pain that immediately follows burns
- ✓ Minimizing the onset of shock
- ✓ Prevention of infection.

Remove all clothing from the injured area, but cut around any clothing that adheres to the skin and leave it in place. Keep the patient covered, except the injured part, since there is a tendency to chill.

First aid dressings for burns and scalds should be free of grease or oil which make it necessary to cleanse the burned or scalded areas with a solvent before medical treatment can begin. This delays the medical treatment and is very painful.

Be careful when dressing burns and scalds. Burned and scalded surfaces are subject to infection the same as open wounds and require the same care to prevent infection. **Do not** break blisters intentionally.

Never permit burned surfaces to be in contact with each other, such as areas between the fingers or toes, the ears and the side of the head, the under surface of the arm and the chest wall, the folds of the groin, and similar places.

Cover bandages should be loose enough to prevent pressure on burned surfaces. Swelling often takes place after burn dressings have been applied, so check them frequently to see that they are not too tight. Watch for evidence of shock and treat if it is present.

In cases of severe burns, remove the victim to the hospital as quickly as possible. The victim will probably require an anesthetic so ordinarily nothing should be given by mouth. In addition to the general principles listed, certain other principles must be followed when giving first aid for specific types of burns.

Chemical Burns of the Eyes

Frequently chemical substances get into the eyes. The treatment is to wash the eyes freely with clean water. To do this, have the victim lie down, hold the eyelids open with the fingers and pour the water into the inner corner of the eyes from a pitcher or other container. Use plenty of water and wash the eyes thoroughly, being sure the water actually flows across the eyes. **Do not** put neutralizing solution in the eyes. Cover both eyes with moistened sterile gauze pads and secure in place. Chemical burns of the eyes should receive the attention of an eye specialist as soon as possible.

Chemical Burns

General first aid for chemical burns is as follows:

- ✓ Remove all clothing containing the chemical agent.
- ✓ **Do not** use any neutralizing solution, unless recommended by a physician.
- ✓ Irrigate with water for at least 15 minutes, use potable water if possible.
- ✓ Treat for shock.
- ✓ Transport to a medical facility.

First aid for dry chemical (alkali) burns is an exception to the general first aid for chemical burns because mixing water with dry alkali creates a corrosive substance. The dry alkali should be brushed from the skin and water should then be used in very large amounts.

Minor Thermal Burns

General first aid for minor thermal burns is as follows:

- ✓ Use cool, moist applications of gauze or bandage material to minimize blistering.
- ✓ Treat for physical shock.

If the victim has thermal burns on the eyelids, apply moist, sterile gauze pads to both eyes and secure in place.

Moderate or Critical Thermal Burns

General first aid for more serious thermal burns is as follows:

- ✓ **Do not** use cold applications on extensive burns; cold could cause chilling.
- ✓ Cover the burn with a clean, dry dressing.
- ✓ Treat for shock.
- ✓ Transport to a medical facility.

Electrical Burns

General first aid for electrical burns is as follows:

- ✓ Conduct a primary survey, as cardiac and respiratory arrest can occur in cases of electrical burns.
- ✓ Check for points of entry and exit of current.
- ✓ Cover burned surface with a clean dressing.
- ✓ Splint all fractures. (Violent muscle contractions caused by the electricity may result in fractures.)
- ✓ Treat for physical shock.
- ✓ Transport to a medical facility.

Respiratory failure and cardiac arrest are the major problems caused by electrical shock and **not** the burn. Monitor pulse and breathing while preparing victim for transportation.

Radiation Burns

Radiation presents a hazard to the rescuer as well as the victim. A rescuer who must enter a radioactive area should stay for as short a time as possible. Radiation is undetectable by the human senses and the rescuer, while attempting to aid the victim, may receive a fatal dose of radiation without realizing it. Notify experts immediately of possible radioactive contamination.

Burns of the Face, Head, and Neck

Any burn of the face is dangerous since it may involve injury to the airway or the eyes. When applying gauze for burns of the face or head, avoid covering the nostrils as the victim may already be having respiratory problems. Victims with respiratory illnesses will be placed in greater jeopardy when exposed to heated air or chemical vapors. Victims with other health problems such as heart disease, kidney disease, or diabetes will react more severely to burn damage. Treat all burns as more serious if accompanied by other injuries.

To dress a burn of the face or head, proceed as follows:

- ✓ Apply several layers of gauze to the burned area and ensure that the gauze is placed between raw surfaces of ears and head.
- ✓ Loosely apply a cravat bandage around the forehead to secure layers of gauze for the upper part of the face.
- ✓ Loosely apply a second cravat bandage around the chin to secure layers of gauze for the lower part of the face.

If the neck only is burned:

- ✓ Dress it by applying gauze or other burn dressing.
- ✓ The burn dressing should be applied in several layers and covered with a cravat bandage the same as for wounds and bleeding of the neck.
- ✓ Burn dressings should always be applied loosely.

Burns to the Back

For burns to the back, apply gauze in several layers and ensure that it covers all burned surfaces including between the arm and chest wall and in the armpit. Cover the gauze dressings with a cover dressing as follows:

- ✓ Split the apex of a triangular bandage just far enough to tie around the front of neck.
- ✓ Place the base of bandage around the lower part of the back and tie in front.
- ✓ Dress small burns of the back loosely with a triangular or cravat bandage as for wounds and bleeding between shoulders or wounds of the back as the injury may indicate.

Burns on the Chest

For burns on the chest, apply gauze in several layers and ensure that it covers all burned surfaces including between the arm and chest wall and in the armpit. Cover the gauze dressing with a cover dressing as follows:

- ✓ Split the apex of a bandage just enough to tie at the back of neck.
- ✓ Place base of bandage around the waist and tie in back.
- ✓ Dress small burns of the chest loosely with a triangular cravat bandage as for wounds and bleeding between the shoulders or wounds of the chest as the injury may indicate.

Treatment of all Other Burns

Burn dressings should be loosely covered with a bandage as described for a wound and bleeding of the part or parts involved.

Sprains, Strains, and Fractures

The musculoskeletal system is composed of all the bones, joints, muscles, tendons, ligaments, and cartilage in the body. The makeup of the musculoskeletal system is subject to injury from sprains, strains, fractures and dislocations.

Sprains

Sprains are injuries due to stretching or tearing ligaments or other tissues at a joint. They are caused by a sudden twist or stretch of a joint beyond normal range of motion.

Sprains may be minor injuries, causing pain and discomfort for only a few hours. In severe cases, however, they may require many weeks of medical care before normal use is restored.

The symptoms of a sprain are:

- Pain on movement
- Swelling
- Tenderness
- Discoloration

Sprains present basically the same signs as a closed fracture. If you cannot determine whether the injury is a fracture or a sprain, treat it as a fracture.

The first aid for sprains is as follows:

- ✓ Elevate the injured area and place it at complete rest.
- ✓ Reduce swelling and relieve pain by applying an ice bag, a cloth wrung in cold water or a chemical cold pack. **Caution: Never use ice in direct contact with the skin; always wrap it in a towel or other material.**
- ✓ If swelling and pain persist, take the victim to the doctor.

The ankle is the part of the body most commonly affected by sprains.

When the ankle has been sprained and the injured person must use the foot temporarily to reach a place for further treatment, the following care should be given:

✓ Unlace the shoe, but do not remove it.
✓ Place the center of a narrow cravat bandage under the foot in front of the heel of the shoe.
✓ Carry the ends up and back of the ankle, crossing above the heel, then forward, crossing over the instep, and then downward toward the arch to make a hitch under the cravat on each side, just in front of the heel of the shoe.
✓ Pull tightly and carry the ends back across the instep.
✓ Tie at the back of the ankle.

Strains

A strain is an injury to a muscle or a tendon caused by overexertion. In severe cases muscles or tendons are torn and the muscle fibers are stretched. Strains are caused by sudden movements or overexertion.

Symptoms of a strain are:

- Intense pain
- Moderate swelling
- Painful and difficult movement
- Sometimes, discoloration

The first aid care for a strain is as follows:

✓ Place the victim in a comfortable position.
✓ Apply a hot, wet towel.
✓ Keep the injured area at rest.
✓ Seek medical attention.

Fractures

A fracture is a broken or cracked bone.

For first aid purposes fractures can be divided into two classifications:

- **Open, or compound fracture**. The bone is broken and an open wound is present. Often the end of the broken bone protrudes from the wound.
- **Closed, or simple fracture**. No open wound is present, but there is a broken or cracked bone.

Broken bones, especially the long bones of the upper and lower extremities, often have sharp edges; even slight movement may cause the sharp edges to cut into blood vessels, nerves, or muscles, and perhaps through the skin. Careless or improper handling can convert a closed fracture into an open fracture, causing damage to surrounding blood vessels or nerves. A person handling a fracture should always keep this in mind. Damage due to careless handling may greatly increase pain and shock, cause complications that will prolong disability, and endanger life through hemorrhage of surrounding blood vessels.

If the broken ends of the bone extend through an open wound, there is little doubt that the victim has suffered a fracture. However, the bone does not always extend through the skin, so the person administering first aid must be able to recognize other signs that a fracture exists.

The general signs and symptoms of a fracture are:

- Pain or tenderness in the region of the fracture
- Deformity or irregularity of the affected area

- Loss of function of the affected area
- Moderate or severe swelling
- Discoloration
- Information from the victim who may have felt the bone snap or break

Be careful when examining injured persons, particularly those apparently suffering from fractures. For all fractures the first aider must remember to maintain an open airway, control bleeding and treat for shock. Do not attempt to change the position of an injured person until he or she has been examined and it has been determined that movement will not complicate the injuries. If the victim is lying down, it is far better to attend to the injuries with the victim in that position and with as little movement as possible. If fractures are present, make any necessary movement in such a manner as to protect the injured part against further injury.

Splints

Use splints to support, immobilize, and protect parts with injuries such as known or suspected fractures, dislocations or severe sprains. When in doubt, treat the injury as a fracture and splint it. Splints prevent movement at the injury and at the nearest joints. Splints should immobilize and support the joint or bones above and below the break.

Many types of splints are available commercially. Easily applied and quickly inflated plastic splints give support to injured limbs. Improvised splints may be made from pieces of wood, broom handles, newspapers, heavy cardboard, boards, magazines, or similar firm materials.

Certain guidelines should be followed when splinting:

✓ Gently remove all clothing from around any suspected fracture or dislocation.

✓ Do not attempt to push bones back through an open wound.

✓ Do not attempt to straighten any fracture.
✓ Cover open wounds with a sterile dressing before applying a splint.
✓ Pad splints with soft material to prevent excessive pressure on the affected area and to aid in supporting the injured part.
✓ Pad under all natural arches of the body such as the knee and wrist.
✓ Support the injured part while splint is applied.
✓ Splint firmly, but not so tightly as to interfere with circulation or cause undue pain.
✓ Support fracture or dislocation before transporting victim.
✓ Elevate injured part and apply ice when possible.

Use inflatable splints to immobilize fractures of the lower leg or forearm. When applying inflatable splints (non–zipper type), follow these guidelines:

✓ Put splint on your own arm so that the bottom edge is above your wrist.
✓ Help support the victim's limb or have someone else hold it.
✓ Hold injured limb, and slide the splint from your forearm over the victim's injured limb.
✓ Inflate by mouth only to the desired pressure. The splint should be inflated to the point where your thumb would make a slight indentation.
✓ Do not use an inflatable plastic splint with an open fracture with protruding bones.

For a zipper–type air splint, lay the victim's limb in the air splint, zip it and inflate. Traction cannot be maintained with this type of splint.

Change in temperature can affect air splints. Going from a cold area to a warm area will cause the splint to expand or vice versa, therefore, it may be necessary to deflate or inflate the splint until proper pressure is reached.

Areas of Fracture

Skull

A fracture may occur to any area of the skull and is considered serious due to possible injury to the brain. Injuries to the back of the head are particularly dangerous since a fractured skull may result without a visible wound to the scalp. The victim of a skull fracture may exhibit any or all of the following symptoms:

- Loss of consciousness for any length of time
- Difficulty in breathing
- Clear or blood–tinged fluid coming from the nose and/or ears
- Partial or complete paralysis
- Pupils of unequal size
- Speech disturbance
- Convulsions
- Vomiting
- Impaired vision or sudden blindness

Consider all serious injuries to the head as possible fractures of the skull. A person with a skull fracture may also have an injury to the neck and spine.

The first aid for a skull fracture is as follows:

✓ Stabilize the head as you open the airway using the modified jaw–thrust maneuver.

✓ Check breathing – restore if necessary.

✓ Check pulse.

✓ Control bleeding from the scalp with minimal pressure and dress the wound; tie the knots of the bandage away from injured area. Do not try to control bleeding from ears or nose.

✓ Keep the victim quiet and lying down.

✓ Maintain an open airway.

✓ Immobilize head, neck, and back on backboard.
✓ Elevate the head end of the stretcher.
✓ Never give a stimulant.
✓ Keep the victim warm and treat for shock.
✓ Pad around fractured area and under neck to keep victim's head from resting on suspected fracture.

Spinal Column

The spinal column consists of bones called vertebrae. Each vertebra surrounds and protects the spinal cord and specific nerve roots.

Fracture of the spinal column may occur at any point along the backbone. Where portions of the broken vertebrae are displaced, the spinal cord may be cut, or pressure may be put on the cord.

Spinal cord injuries can result in paralysis or death, because they cannot always be corrected by surgery and the spinal cord has very limited self healing powers. Thus, it is extremely important for the person giving first aid to be able to recognize the signs of spinal column damage.

The following signs and symptoms are associated with spinal injuries:

- Pain and tenderness at the site of the injury
- Deformity
- Cuts and bruises
- Paralysis.

First, check the lower extremities for paralysis. If the victim is conscious, use the following method:

✓ Ask the victim if he or she can feel your touch on his or her feet.
✓ Ask the victim to wiggle his or her toes.

✓ Ask the victim to press against your hand with his or her feet.

Second, check the upper extremities for paralysis. If the victim is conscious, use the following method:

✓ Ask the victim if he or she can feel your touch to his or her hands.

✓ Ask the victim to wiggle his or her fingers.

✓ Ask the victim to grasp your hand and squeeze.

If the victim is unconscious, perform the following tests:

✓ Stroke soles of feet or ankles with a pointed object; if the spinal cord is undamaged, the feet will react.

✓ Stroke palms of the hands with a pointed object; if the spinal cord is undamaged, the hands will react.

Treat all questionable injuries to the spinal column, even in the absence of signs of paralysis, as a fracture of the spinal column. The initial care that the victim receives at the scene of the accident is extremely important. Proper care, not speed, is essential. Improper care or handling could result in paralysis or death.

First aid for an individual with a fractured spinal column uses fifteen bandages as follows:

✓ If a broken–back splint is used, pad each long board with a blanket.

✓ Stabilize the head, immobilizing it in line with the rest of the body. Maintain stabilization until after the victim is secured to a splint, stretcher, or other hard, flat surface which provides firm support. Do not move victim until completely immobilized.

✓ Use a blanket or padding around the head and neck. Fold to make a strip about six inches wide and long enough to run along the side of the head from the shoulder to the head, across the top of the head and down the other side to the shoulder.

✓ Pass first bandage around the forehead padding and splint, and tie on the outer side of splint.

- ✓ Pass second bandage around the splint and padding at the chin, and tie on the outer side of splint.
- ✓ Pass third bandage around the body and well up in the armpits and tie on outer side of splint.
- ✓ Pass fourth bandage around the body and splint at the lower part of the chest and tie on the outer side of the splint.
- ✓ Pass the fifth bandage around the body and splint at the hips, and tie on the outer side of the splint.
- ✓ Pass the center of the sixth bandage well up on the shoulder, passing one end between the long boards under the neck, continuing under crosspiece, completing tie at the upper edge of splint under armpit.
- ✓ Tie the seventh bandage in the same manner around the other shoulder.
- ✓ Pass the eighth bandage around one hip and crotch and crosspiece between long boards and tie on outer side of splint.
- ✓ Apply ninth bandage in the same manner around the other hip.
- ✓ Apply tenth bandage around the upper part of one thigh and the long board and tie on the outer side of the splint.
- ✓ Apply eleventh bandage on the other side in the same manner.
- ✓ Pass twelfth bandage around the leg and long board just below the knee and tie on the outer side of the splint.
- ✓ Apply thirteenth bandage on the other side in the same manner.
- ✓ Pass fourteenth bandage around one ankle and the long board, and tie on the outer side of the splint.
- ✓ Apply fifteenth bandage on the other side in the same manner.
- ✓ Use enough people to safely lift the victim as a unit

and place the victim on his or her back on the splint or stretcher.
✓ Lift victim only high enough to slide the splint or stretcher underneath.
✓ Secure the victim to the splint or stretcher so that the entire body is immobilized.
✓ Cover with a blanket and treat for shock.

Nose

A broken nose is a very common type of fracture and may result from any hard blow. The symptoms of a broken nose are as follows:

- Deformity of the bridge of the nose
- Pain
- Bleeding
- Swelling

Treat any blow to the nose that causes bleeding as a fracture. The first aid care for a broken nose is as follows:
✓ Apply a bandage compress if an open fracture.
✓ Take the victim to the doctor.

Upper Jaw

In fractures of the upper jaw or cheekbone, where there is an open wound, treat as for an open wound of the face, but do not tie bandage knots over wounds. If there is no open wound, a dressing is not necessary, but take the victim to a doctor.

Lower Jaw

The symptoms of a fracture of the lower jaw are:

- The mouth is usually open
- Saliva mixed with blood flows from the mouth
- The teeth of the lower jaw may be uneven, loosened, or knocked out
- Talking is painful and difficult

The first aid for a fracture of the lower jaw is as follows:

- ✓ Maintain a clear airway.
- ✓ Gently place the jaw in a position so that the lower teeth rest against the upper teeth, if possible.
- ✓ Place the center of a cravat bandage over the front of the chin and pass the ends around the back of the head and tie, leaving the ends long.
- ✓ Place center of a second cravat bandage under the chin, pass the ends over the cheeks to the center of the top of the head and tie, leaving ends long.
- ✓ Bring the ends of the two bandages together and tie separately. Do not tie too tightly.
- ✓ Transport the victim on his or her side to allow drainage if no spinal injury is suspected.

Collarbone

Fracture of the collarbone frequently is caused by a fall with the hand outstretched or by a blow to the shoulder. The symptoms of a fractured collarbone are:

- Pain in the area of the shoulder
- Partial or total disability of the arm on the injured side
- The injured shoulder tends to droop forward
- The victim frequently supports the arm on the injured side at the elbow or wrist with the other hand

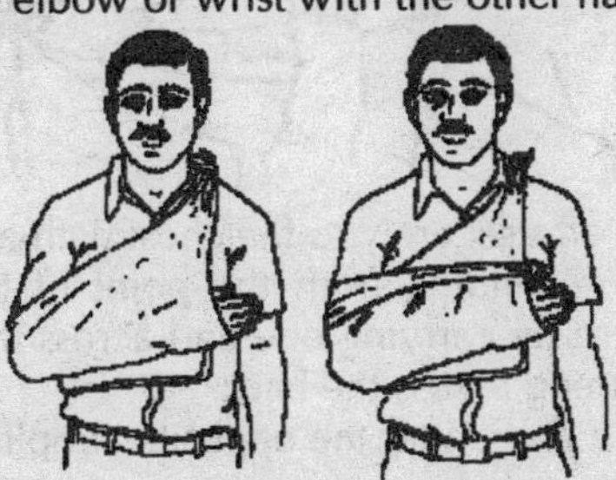

Support the fracture until the following dressings have been applied:

✓ Place padding between arm and the victim's side.
✓ Put the arm on the injured side in a triangular sling with the hand elevated about four to five inches.
✓ Secure arm on the injured side to the body with a medium cravat. Center bandage on the outside of the arm. Carry bandage across the chest and back. Tie over a pad on the uninjured side of the body.

Shoulder Blade

Fracture of the shoulder blade is not common. It is sometimes caused by a direct blow to the shoulder blade and usually results in a closed fracture with little displacement. Symptoms are pain and swelling at the fracture and inability to swing the arm back and forth from the shoulder.
To support a fracture of shoulder blade proceed as follows:
✓ Place the forearm in a triangular sling.

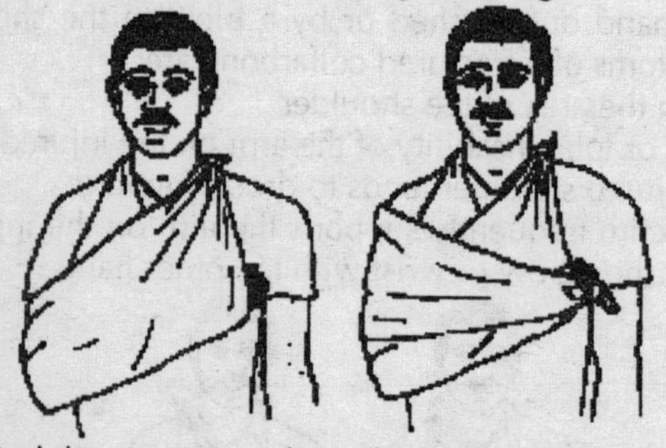

✓ Bind the arm securely to the chest with a wide cravat bandage extending from the point of the shoulder downward by carrying one end across the chest and the other end across the back.
✓ Tie over a pad under the opposite armpit.

Upper Arm

Fracture of the upper portion of the arm is recognized by the following symptoms: swelling; deformity; inability to use the arm below the point of the fracture.

In order to immobilize a fracture of the upper third of the arm proceed as follows:

- ✓ Have an assistant support the fracture on both sides of the break.
- ✓ Bind arm to the rib cage with a wide cravat bandage tied over a pad under the opposite armpit.

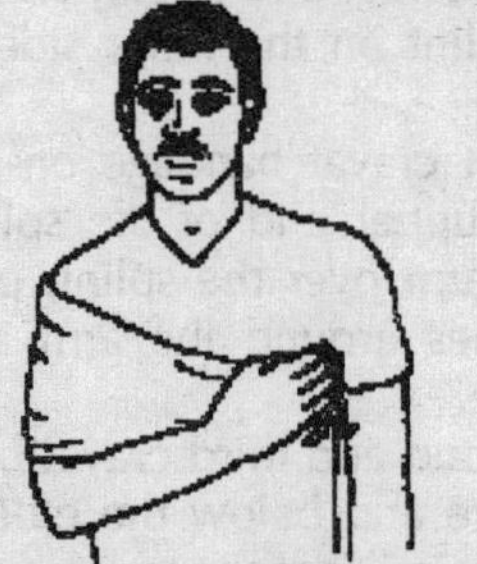

- ✓ Place the forearm in a cravat bandage sling.

Do not pull the forearm up too high because this will increase pain.

Lower Arm, Elbow, Forearm, or Wrist

Take extreme care when dealing with a fractured elbow, as the fracture may cause extensive damage to surrounding tissues, nerves, and blood vessels. Improper care and handling of a fractured elbow could result in a permanent disability.

The symptoms of a fractured elbow are:

- Extreme pain
- Extensive discoloration around elbow

- Swelling
- Deformity
- Bone may be visible or projecting from the wound

The first aid for a fractured elbow in a straight position is as follows:

✓ Do not bend, straighten, or twist the arm in any direction.

✓ If available, apply an inflatable plastic splint.

✓ If an inflatable plastic splint is not available, use a splint long enough to reach from one inch below armpit to one inch beyond tip of the middle finger.

✓ While fracture is being supported, pad to conform to the deformity and place splint on the inner side of the arm.

✓ Place the center of the first cravat bandage on the outside of the arm at the upper end of the splint, cross on the inside of the arm over the splint, pass the ends one or more times around the arm and splint, and tie on the outside.

✓ Place the centers of the second and third cravat bandages on the arm just above and below the elbow, and apply in a similar manner.

✓ Center the fourth cravat bandage on the back of the wrist. Pass the ends around and cross on the splint under the wrist, bring one end up around the little finger side, and cross over the back of the hand and down between the forefinger and thumb. Pass the other end up over the thumb, cross it over the back of the hand down around the little finger side, then cross both ends on the splint and tie on top of the hand.

✓ Tie a fifth cravat bandage around splint, arm and body to prevent movement during transportation.

If the arm is bent, immobilize in a bent position by making an L–shaped splint for the forearm and wrist from two pieces of board one–half inch thick and four inches wide. One piece should be long enough to extend from one inch below the armpit to the point of the elbow and the other long enough to extend from the point of the elbow to one inch beyond the end of the middle finger. Immobilize the limb to the splint in the following manner:

- ✓ Fasten the boards together securely to form an L–shaped splint.
- ✓ Pad the splint.
- ✓ While an assistant supports the fracture on both sides of the break apply the splint to the inner side of the arm and forearm after placing the forearm across the chest.
- ✓ Use four cravat bandages to hold splint in place.
- ✓ Place the center of the first cravat bandage on the outside of the arm at the upper end of the splint, pass around arm one or more times, and tie on the arm.
- ✓ Place the centers of second and third cravat bandages on arm and forearm, respectively, passing around one or more times and tying on the arm.
- ✓ Apply fourth cravat bandage by placing the center of the bandage on the back of the wrist, passing the ends around and crossing on the splint under the wrist. Take one end up around the little finger side, passing over back of the hand and down between the forefinger and thumb. Pass the other end up over the thumb, and cross it over back of the hand down around the little finger side; then cross both ends on the splint and tie on top of the hand.
- ✓ Place the arm in a cravat bandage sling.

Fractures of the forearm and wrist are usually less painful than fractures of the arm, shoulder blade, or elbow. The symptoms of a fractured forearm and wrist are as follows: pain; tenderness; severe deformity, especially if both bones of the forearm are broken.

If available, use a plastic inflatable splint to immobilize the forearm or wrist.

Hand and Fingers

Fractures of the hand usually result from a direct blow. The symptoms of a fracture of the hand are as follows: acute pain; tenderness; swelling; discoloration; enlarged joints.

If available, use a plastic inflatable splint for immobilization.

Use a board splint if a plastic inflatable splint is not available. To immobilize a fractured hand with a board splint, proceed as follows:

- ✓ Apply a well–padded splint about one–half inch thick, four inches wide, and long enough to reach from the point of the elbow to one inch beyond the end of the middle finger.
- ✓ Place padding in palm of the hand and under wrist.
- ✓ Carry one end around little finger side across the back of the hand and wrist and other end around thumb side across the back of the hand and wrist.
- ✓ Cross the ends on the inside of the wrist, bring them to the back of the wrist and tie.
- ✓ Bring the apex down over the knot and tuck under.
- ✓ Place the forearm in a cravat bandage sling.
- ✓ Apply the splint to the inside of the forearm and hand with one cravat and one triangular bandage.
- ✓ Place the center of the cravat on the outside of the forearm just below the elbow; pass it around the

forearm one or more times; tie it on the outside of the forearm.

- ✓ Place the base of a triangular bandage under the splint at the wrist; bring the apex around the end of the splint over the hand to a point above the wrist.
- ✓ Carry one end around the little finger side across back of the hand and wrist and other end around the thumb side across back of the hand and wrist.
- ✓ Cross the ends on the inside of the wrist, bring them to the back of the wrist and tie.
- ✓ Bring the apex down over the knot and tuck under.
- ✓ Place the forearm in a cravat bandage sling.

Finger

The symptoms of a fracture of the finger is as follows: pain; swelling; deformity.

The first aid for a fractured finger is as follows:

- ✓ Place a narrow padded splint under the broken finger and palm of the hand.
- ✓ Pass a narrow strip of cloth around the splint and palm of the hand; tie over the splint.
- ✓ Pass a narrow strip of cloth around the finger and the splint above the fracture; tie over the splint.
- ✓ Pass a narrow strip of cloth around the finger and the splint below the fracture; tie over the splint.
- ✓ Place the hand in a narrow cravat bandage sling.

Rib

Fracture of a rib usually is caused by a direct blow or a severe squeeze. A fracture can occur at any point along the rib. The symptoms of a fractured rib are as follows: severe pain on breathing; tenderness over the fracture; deformity; inability to take a deep breath.

Cravat bandages will immobilize fractured ribs. Place the bandages in the following order:

- ✓ Apply padding over injured ribs.

✓ Apply two medium cravat bandages around the chest firmly enough to afford support, centering the cravats on either side of the pain.

✓ Upon exhalation, tie the knots over a pad on the opposite side of the body. If the cravat bandages cause more pain, loosen them.

✓ Support the arm on the injured side in a sling.

✓ Treat for shock as it is usually severe.

✓ Secure medical treatment.

Wrap the chest gently when the ribs are depressed or frothy blood comes from the victim's mouth. These may be indications of a punctured lung. Place the victim in a semi–prone position (if no neck or spine injury exists) with the injured side down. This will allow more room for expansion of the uninjured lung.

Pelvis or Hip

Fracture of the pelvis or hip usually results from a squeezing type injury through the hips or from a direct blow. Use extreme care when handling an individual with a fracture of the pelvis or hip because there is a possibility of associated internal injuries to the digestive, urinary, or genital organs. The symptoms of a fractured pelvis or hip are: pain in the pelvic region; discoloration; unable to raise his or her leg; inward rotation of foot and leg on affected side.

To support the pelvic region before the victim is transported proceed as follows:

✓ Maintain support of the pelvic region with hands at the sides of the hips until two wide bandages have been applied.

✓ Place the center of a wide cravat bandage over one hip, the upper edge extending about two inches above the crest of the hip bone.

- ✓ Pass the ends around the body and tie over a pad on the opposite hip.
- ✓ Place the center of a second wide cravat bandage over the opposite hip, the upper edge extending about two inches above the crest of the hipbone.
- ✓ Pass the ends around the body and tie on the first bandage.
- ✓ Lift victim only high enough to place him or her on a firm support, preferably a broken back splint.

When a broken back splint is used, secure body to the splint with eight cravat bandages as follows:

- ✓ Pass the first cravat bandage around the splint and the upper part of the chest, well up in the armpits and tie on one side near the splint.
- ✓ Pass second cravat bandage around the splint and the lower part of the chest and tie near the splint.
- ✓ Pass the third and fourth cravat bandages around the splint and each thigh just below the crotch and tie on the outside near the splint.
- ✓ Pass the fifth and sixth cravat bandages around splint and each leg, just below the knee and tie on the outside near the splint.
- ✓ Pass the seventh and eighth cravat bandages around the splint and each ankle, and tie on the outside near the splint.
- ✓ Cover the victim with a blanket and treat for shock.
- ✓ Get the victim to the doctor or hospital.

Thigh or Knee

If a fracture of the thigh or knee is open, dress the wound. If the fracture is at the knee joint and the limb is not in a straight position, make no attempt to straighten the limb. Splint in line of deformity. Attempts to straighten the limb may increase the possibility of permanent damage. Improvise a way to immobilize knee as it is found, using padding to fill any space. Use the utility splint stretcher or a similar support to immobilize fractures of the knee or thigh.

Before placing the victim on the stretcher, it should be well padded and tested. Additional padding will also be necessary for the natural arches of the body. Raise the victim carefully for placement on the stretcher while the fracture is supported from the underside on both sides of the break.

Apply the splint with bandages. All bandages should be tied on the injured side near the splint.

- ✓ Tie the first bandage around the body and splint under the armpits.
- ✓ Tie the second around the chest and splint and the third around the hips and splint.
- ✓ Tie the fourth and fifth bandages on the injured leg just below the crotch at the thigh and above the knee, respectively, (above and below fracture) and tie on the injured side near the splint.
- ✓ Tie the sixth and seventh bandages on the injured leg below the knee and at the ankle.
- ✓ An additional bandage at the ankle on the uninjured side may be needed for additional support.
- ✓ The victim should be transported on a regular stretcher or stretcher board.

When using a stretcher board, it should be well padded and the bandages applied in normal order. On some types of stretcher boards it may be necessary to tie both lower limbs together with each of the last four cravat bandages. To prevent movement of the legs, pad well between the legs before applying the cravats.

Any improvised splint for the thigh or knee should be long enough to immobilize the hip and the ankle.

Kneecap

A splint suitable for a broken back may also be used for a fracture of the kneecap. Dress any open wound first. The splint should be well padded with additional padding under all natural body arches. Support the fracture from the top and on both sides and carefully raise the victim to place the prepared and tested splint underneath.

Apply the splint with seven cravat bandages. Tie all bandages on the injured side near the splint, except the fifth and sixth bandages which tie on top.

- ✓ Tie three bandages around the body and the splint; one just below the armpits, one around the chest, and one around the hips.
- ✓ Tie the fourth bandage around the thigh and splint just below the crotch.
- ✓ Place center of fifth bandage just above the kneecap, bring the ends under the thigh and splint, and bring ends over leg above kneecap, but do not tie.
- ✓ Place the center of the sixth bandage just below the kneecap, bring ends under the leg and splint, up over thigh and tie above knee over fifth bandage.
- ✓ Pull the ends of the fifth bandage tight and tie below the knee over the sixth bandage.
- ✓ The seventh bandage is tied around the ankle and splint.
- ✓ An additional bandage at ankle and thigh on uninjured side may be needed for additional support.

Transport the victim on a regular stretcher. Any stretcher board used for this type of injury should be the type of board which is prepared for individual bandaging of each lower extremity. Otherwise, the bandages would be applied as for fracture of thigh or knee. Any improvised splint for the kneecap should be long enough to immobilize the hip and the ankle.

Leg or Ankle

If the fracture is open, dress the wound before splinting. When it is necessary to remove a shoe or boot because of pain from swelling of the ankle or for any other reason, the removal must be carefully done by unlacing or cutting the boot to prevent damage to the ankle. In the absence of severe swelling or bleeding it may be wise to leave the boot on for additional support.

The splint for a fracture of the leg or ankle should reach from against the buttocks to beyond the heel. Place a well–padded splint under the victim while the leg is supported on both sides of the fracture. Tie the bandages on the outer side, near the splint as follows:

- ✓ Pass the end of the first bandage around the inner side of the thigh at the groin, pass it over the thigh under the splint, and tie.
- ✓ Pass two bandages around the thigh and splint, one at the middle of the thigh and the other just above the knee and tie.
- ✓ Place additional padding around knee and ankle.
- ✓ Place a padded splint on the outer side of the leg.
- ✓ Pass a fourth bandage around the leg, the padding, and the splint just below the knee and tie; pass a fifth bandage just above or below the fracture and tie. **Do not** tie over fracture.
- ✓ Pass the center of a sixth bandage around the instep and bring the ends up each side of the ankle.
- ✓ Cross the ends on top and pass them around the ankle and splint.
- ✓ Cross the ends under the splint, return to the top of the ankle, cross and carry down each side of the ankle and tie under the instep.

When using an inflatable plastic splint, roll up or cut away the clothing from the limb to a point above the upper end of the splint. The splint should be long enough to immobilize the knee as well as the ankle. Cover open wounds with gauze, but they need not be bandaged because the splint will form an airtight cover for such wounds. After the splint is applied, pressure from the inflated splint will help control any bleeding that may develop. Apply the splint while supporting the fracture on both sides. Close and inflate the splint.

Ankle or Foot

To make an improvised splint for the ankle or foot, proceed as follows:

- ✓ Carefully fold a blanket or pillow around the ankle and foot.
- ✓ Tie first bandage around the leg above the ankle.
- ✓ Tie the second bandage around the ankle.
- ✓ Tie the third bandage below the ankle.
- ✓ Place padding between the ankles and extend the padding above the knees.
- ✓ Place the fourth bandage around knees and tie.
- ✓ Place the fifth bandage below knees and tie.
- ✓ Place the sixth bandage around ankles and tie.

Crushed Bones of Foot or Toes

When caring for a fracture of the foot or toes, leave a boot or shoe in place if possible and support the injured foot. Use extreme care if it is necessary to remove any type of footwear. If a damaged protective cap of a safety boot has become embedded in the foot, do not remove the boot.

It should be noted that it may be impossible to use an inflatable splint with the shoe on. If footwear is removed, carefully dress any open wounds before applying a splint.

Immobilize a fracture of the foot or toes as follows:

- ✓ Place a well–padded splint, about four inches wide and long enough to extend from one–half inch beyond the heel to one–half inch beyond the big toe,

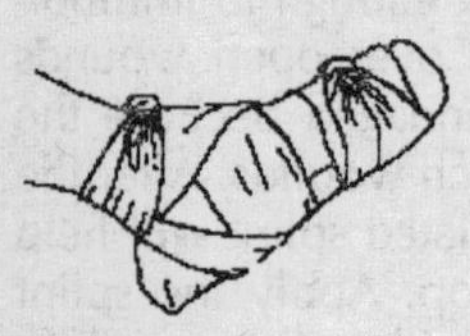

on the bottom of the foot.

✓ Start the center of a cravat bandage around the ankle from the back just above the heel. Cross over the arch and carry under the foot and splint. Cross under the splint and bring the ends to the back of the heel. Cross at the back of the heel, carry the ends around the ankle and tie in front.

✓ Start the center of a second bandage on top of the toes, carry the ends around the foot and splint several times, then tie on top of the foot.

An air splint specifically made for the foot and ankle or an improvised splint made from a blanket or pillow as in caring for a fractured ankle may be used.

Dislocations

Where two or more bones come together they form a joint. The bones forming a joint are held in place by bands of strong, fibrous tissue known as ligaments. There are three varieties of joints: immovable joints, joints with limited motion, and freely movable joints. The first aider is concerned particularly with the freely movable joints—the lower jaw, the shoulders, the elbows, the wrists, the fingers, the hips, the knees, the ankles, and the toes. These are the joints most commonly dislocated.

A dislocation is when one or more of the bones forming a joint slip out of normal position. The ligaments holding the bones in proper position are stretched and sometimes torn loose. Fractures are often associated with dislocations.

Dislocations may result from: force applied at or near the joint; sudden muscular contractions; twisting strains on joint ligaments; falls where the force of landing is transferred to a joint.

General signs of dislocations are: rigidity and loss of function; deformity; pain; swelling; tenderness; discoloration.

General First Aid for Dislocations

A first aider does not have the skill necessary to reduce dislocations. Inexperience in manipulating the joints can further damage the ligaments, blood vessels and nerves found close to joints. With one exception (the lower jaw) only a physician should reduce a dislocation. The victim experiences pain which justifies one reduction attempt.

Splint and/or dress the affected joint in line of deformity in which you find it. Obtain medical help.

Lower Jaw

The symptoms of a dislocated lower jaw are as follows: pain; open mouth; rigid jaw; difficulty in speaking.

If medical aid is not available for some time, reduce the dislocation as follows:

- ✓ Place thumbs in the victim's mouth, resting them well back on each side of the lower teeth.
- ✓ Seize the outside of the lower jaw with the fingers. Press first downward and forward.
- ✓ When the jaw starts into place, slip the thumbs off the teeth to the inside of the cheeks.
- ✓ Remove thumbs from mouth.
- ✓ Place the center of a cravat bandage over the front of the chin.
- ✓ Carry the ends to the back of the head and tie.
- ✓ Center another bandage under the victim's chin, bring the ends to the top of the head and tie.
- ✓ Bring the ends of both bandages together and tie them separately.

NOTE: If the reduction attempt is not successful, do not make repeated attempts to reduce the dislocation and do not apply a dressing. Secure medical treatment.

Shoulder

The shoulder joint usually is dislocated by falls or blows directly on the shoulder or by falls on the hand or elbow. The symptoms of a dislocated shoulder are as follows:

- Elbow stands off one or two inches from the body
- Arm is held rigid
- Shoulder appears flat
- Marked depression beneath the point of the shoulder
- Pain and swelling are present at the site of the injury
- Victim cannot bring the elbow in contact with the side

While the arm is being supported in the position in which it was found, immobilize the shoulder in the following manner:

✓ Place the point of a wedge–shaped pad (approximately four inches wide and one to three inches thick) between the arm and the body.

✓ Tape or tie the pad in place.

✓ Place the center of a medium width cravat on the outside of the arm just above the elbow.

✓ Carry one end across the chest and the other end across the back.

✓ Tie on the opposite side over a pad.

✓ Place the arm in a triangular bandage sling.

Elbow

Dislocation occurs at the elbow joint as a result of a blow at the joint or occasionally by a fall on the hand. It usually can be recognized by these symptoms:

- Deformity at the joint
- Inability to bend the limb at the joint
- Great pain

The elbow must be immobilized in the line the deformity is found.

While the elbow is being supported, proceed as follows:

- ✓ Prepare and pad a splint—straight, L–shaped, or a modification depending on position of arm—long enough to reach from one inch below the armpit to one inch beyond the tip of the middle finger.
- ✓ Pad splint to conform to the deformity, and place on the inside of the arm.
- ✓ Place the center of the first cravat bandage on the outside of the arm at the upper end of the splint, cross on the inside of the arm over the splint, pass the ends one or more times around the arm and splint, and tie on the outside.
- ✓ Place center of the second cravat bandage on arm just above elbow and apply in a similar manner.
- ✓ Place the center of the third cravat bandage on the forearm just below the elbow, and apply in a similar manner.
- ✓ Place the center of the fourth cravat bandage on the back of the wrist, passing the ends around and crossing on the splint under the wrist, bring one end up around the little finger side, and cross over the back of the hand and down between the forefinger and thumb. Pass the other end up over the thumb, cross it over the back of the hand down around the little finger side, then cross both ends on the splint and tie on the top of the hand.
- ✓ Bind limb to the body or place forearm in a cravat bandage sling (depending on position of the arm).

Wrist

Dislocation of the wrist usually occurs when the hand is extended to break a fall. It is difficult, however, to distinguish between a dislocation and a fractured wrist. Treat a suspected dislocated wrist the same as a fractured wrist.

Finger

The usual symptoms of a dislocated finger are:

- Inability to bend at dislocation
- Deformity of the joint
- Shortening of the digit
- Pain and swelling

Do not attempt to reduce the dislocation. immobilize the digit by using small pads as for any deformity and splinting, or by tying the injured member to the one next to it. Obtain medical treatment.

Hip

Dislocation of the hip usually results from falling onto the foot or knee. It may also be caused by a direct blow when the thigh is at an angle with the spine. While supporting the dislocation in the line of deformity, carefully raise the victim only high enough to be placed on a well–padded and tested splint or stretcher board suitable for a broken back. Support is necessary until the splint or stretcher board is applied.

Symptoms of a dislocated hip are:

- Intense pain
- Lengthening or shortening of the leg, with foot turned in or out
- Pain and swelling at the joint

The first aid for a dislocated hip is:

- ✓ Make a pad of clothing, blankets, or other material large enough to support the limb in the line of deformity. (The affected leg will be turned either inward or outward.)
- ✓ Place a small pad between the feet.
- ✓ Pass the first cravat bandage around the splint, the upper part of the chest, and tie the ends of the bandage on the injured side near the splint.
- ✓ Pass the second cravat bandage around the splint

and lower part of the chest and tie the ends of the bandage on the injured side near the splint.

✓ Pass third cravat bandage around splint and body at the hips, and tie on injured side near the splint.

✓ Pass the fourth cravat bandage around the splint and the thigh just above the knee, and tie on the injured side near the splint.

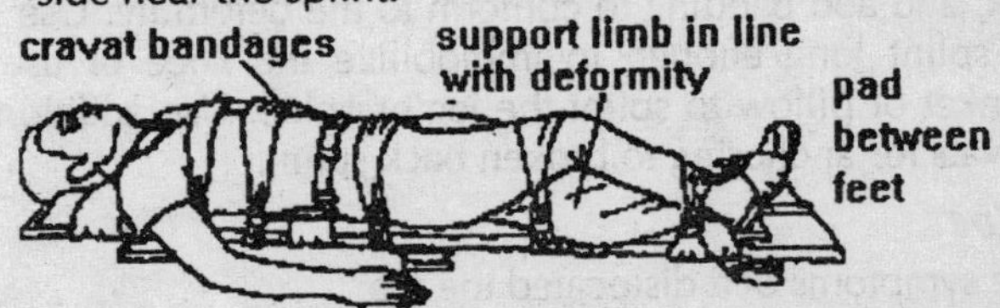

✓ Pass fifth cravat bandage around the splint and the ankles, and tie on the injured side near the splint.

✓ Pass the sixth cravat bandage over the insteps, cross the ends under the soles of the feet, and bring them back to the insteps, tying loosely.

✓ If the victim is unconscious, the forearms should be placed in a basket sling.

Knee

Dislocation of the knee results from direct force applied at the knee or from a fall on the knee. The symptoms of the dislocation are as follows:

- Deformity
- Inability to use the knee
- Great pain

While supporting the dislocation, apply a splint as for fracture of the thigh, using either a broken back splint or a stretcher board. Place extra padding of blankets, clothes, or similar material to conform to the deformity.

Ankle

Dislocation of the ankle may show several types of deformity. Bones are almost always broken. There is a marked deformity at the joint. As a rule, there is rapid and marked swelling and great pain. While supporting the dislocation, apply an improvised splint as for a fracture of the ankle or foot, and add padding to conform to the deformity. Use an air splint long enough to immobilize the knee or use a blanket or pillow to splint the leg or ankle. Use additional cravats for anchoring to broken back splint.

Toe

The symptoms of a dislocated toe are:

- Inability to bend at dislocation
- Deformity of the joint
- Shortening of the digit
- Pain and swelling

Do not attempt to reduce the dislocation. Immobilize the digit by using small pads as for any deformity and splinting it by tying the injured member to the one next to it.

Transporting the Injured

After receiving first aid, an injured person often requires transportation to a medical facility. Under special circumstances, such as an accident that takes place in the woods, the victim needs to be transported to a place accessible to ambulance personnel. The first aider is responsible in such cases for seeing that the victim is transported in such a manner as to prevent further injury and not subjected to additional pain or discomfort.

Improper handling and careless transportation may add to original injuries, increase chance of shock, and serve to endanger life.

Under normal circumstances, **do not** move a victim until a thorough examination has been made and first aid has been given. Move a seriously injured person in a position that is least likely to aggravate injuries.

Various methods for carrying a victim can bè used in emergencies, but the stretcher is the preferred method of transportation. Use other means of transportation when a stretcher is unavailable or impractical.

Two-Person Seat Carry

The two-person seat carry is a technique for transporting a victim in a seat fashioned from the rescuers' arms. It provides for speedy removal and can be used when the victim must be moved through narrow passageways.

Do not use this technique when there is indication of damage to the spinal column or any injury that could be aggravated by such handling of the victim.

Three-Person Carry

Use three-person lift and carry to move an injured person a short distance, through narrow passageways, or when a stretcher is not available. Also use this lift when an injured person is being placed on or removed from a stretcher.

This lift requires three persons, and a fourth is desirable. Lifting must be done on command of one person.

To perform three-person lift and carry, proceed as follows:

- ✓ Three rescuers kneel beside the victim on the least injured side, if possible.
- ✓ One bearer, opposite the victim's shoulders, supports the victim's neck and shoulders.
- ✓ One bearer, opposite the victim's hips, supports the victim's thighs and small of the back.
- ✓ The other bearer, opposite the victim's knees, supports the victim's knees and ankles.
- ✓ On command, the bearers slowly lift, keeping the victim's body level, until they can come to rest on the knee nearest the victim's feet.
- ✓ On command, the bearers slowly raise the victim on his or her side so that the victim rests in the bend of their elbows and is held closely to their chests.
- ✓ When the command is given, all bearers should rise in unison.
- ✓ Bearers can then, when commanded, move the victim as carefully as possible.

Four-Person Log Roll

This technique for moving a person with spinal injuries onto a long board requires four persons, one who acts as captain. To perform the four-person log roll, proceed as follows:

- ✓ The rescuer who is acting as captain applies stabilization to the neck and head as he or she opens the airway using the modified jaw-thrust maneuver.

- ✓ Place a stretcher board parallel to the victim.
- ✓ Three rescuers (one at the shoulders, one at the waist, and one at the knees) kneel at the victim's side opposite the board, leaving room to roll the victim towards them while one rescuer maintains stabilization of the neck and head.
- ✓ The shoulder level rescuer extends the victim's arm over the head on the side to which the victim will be rolled (the side toward the rescuers).
- ✓ The shoulder level rescuer then reaches across the victim and places one hand under the victim's shoulder and the other hand under the victim's upper arm.
- ✓ The waist level rescuer reaches across and places one hand on the victim's waist and the other hand under the victim's buttocks.
- ✓ The knee level rescuer reaches across and places one hand under the victim's knees and the other hand under the mid calf.
- ✓ The command is given to roll the victim as a unit onto his or her side.
- ✓ The command is given for the waist level rescuer or bystander to pull a spine board into position against the victim.
- ✓ Command is given to roll the victim in unison onto the stretcher board.
- ✓ Place rolled blankets beside the head and neck for additional protection and secure head to the board with cravat bandages.
- ✓ Secure the victim to the splint or stretcher so that the entire body is immobilized.

Straddle Slide

Another technique for moving a person with a spinal injury onto a long board is the straddle slide. Three persons handle the victim and the fourth person slides the board into place. To perform the straddle slide move, proceed as follows:

- ✓ One rescuer, standing at the head of the victim, bending at the waist, maintains an open airway with the modified jaw-thrust and applies stabilization to the neck and head.
- ✓ The second rescuer straddles the victim, facing toward the head. Bending at the waist, the rescuer grips the victim's arms just below the shoulders.
- ✓ A third rescuer also faces and straddles the victim. Bending at the waist, the rescuer places his or her hands on the sides of the victim's waist. (The legs of the three rescuers must be spread sufficiently to allow passage of the long board between them.)
- ✓ A fourth rescuer positions the board at the victim's head in line with his or her body.
- ✓ On a signal from the commanding rescuer, the rescuers lift the victim just high enough to allow the fourth rescuer to slide the board under victim.
- ✓ On command, the rescuers gently lower the victim onto the board. Support must be maintained until the victim is secured.

Stretchers

Test any stretcher to determine serviceability immediately before placing an injured person on it. Place an uninjured person, weighing as much or more than the victim, face down on the stretcher. Lift the stretcher waist high and lower it to the ground. Pad stretcher with a blanket or similar material after it has been tested. Due to possible deterioration of canvas stretchers, take extra precautionary measures when testing the stretcher.

Canvas Stretcher

The canvas stretcher consists of canvas stretched between two poles. The poles are long enough to afford handholds for the bearers at each end.

Basket Stretcher

Various types of basket stretchers are also used to transport the injured.

After the victim has been secured by means of straps and foot braces, the basket may be transported even in a vertical position.

Stretcher Board or Spine Board

A stretcher board or spine board is made from a wide board approximately one and one-half inches thick, or from laminated plywood about three-quarters of an inch thick. The length is usually about seventy-eight inches and the width eighteen inches. Slots about one inch wide are placed along the edges. Pass cravat bandages through these slots to secure the victim to the board. The slots also serve as handholds. Some variations have additional slots in the center of the boards so that each leg may be secured separately to the board.

There is an aluminum version of the stretcher that is similar to the wooden board except that it folds in half.

Scoop Stretcher

The scoop stretcher is another means for lifting and transporting a victim. Because of its two piece construction, its prime advantage is a minimum of body movement in placing the victim on the stretcher.

Both sides of the victim must be accessible to use this type of stretcher. Slide the frame halves under the victim from either side. Prevent pinching the victim or catching the clothing between the stretcher halves by lifting the victim by the clothes as the stretcher is being closed.

In cases of spinal injury, pelvis, hip, or thigh fractures, use a spine board or broken-back splint.

Improvised Stretchers

A satisfactory stretcher may be improvised with a blanket, canvas, or a strong sheet, and two poles or pieces of pipe, seven to eight feet long. To construct an improvised stretcher using two poles and a blanket, proceed as follows:

- ✓ Place one pole about one foot from the center of the unfolded blanket.
- ✓ Fold the short side of the blanket over the pole.
- ✓ Place second pole on the two thicknesses of blanket

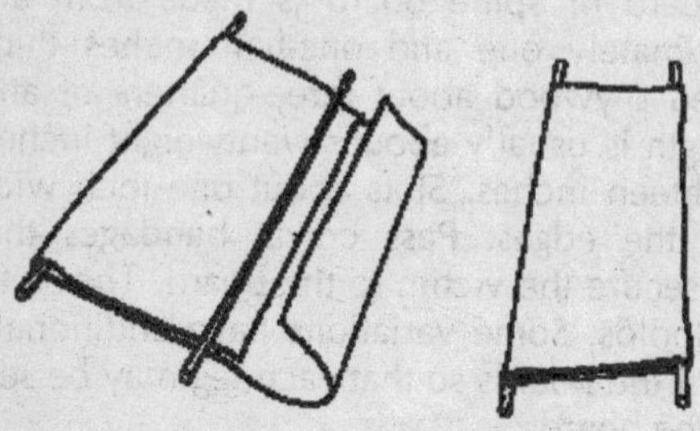

  about two feet from first pole and parallel to it.
- ✓ Fold the remaining side of the blanket over the second pole. When the victim is placed on the blanket, the weight of the body secures the folds.

Use cloth bags or sacks for stretcher beds. Make holes in the bottoms of the bags or sacks, and pass the poles through them. Use enough bags or sacks to give the required length of the bed.

A stretcher can also be made from three or four coats or jackets. Turn the sleeves inside out with the jacket fastened and the sleeves inside the coat. Place a pole through every sleeve on each side.

Stretcher Transportation

When transporting a victim on a canvas stretcher, take care to see that the crosspieces are locked in place.

When lifting a victim for stretcher transportation it is preferable to have four or more persons to lift. If only four persons are available and a spinal injury is not suspected, the following method is recommended:

- ✓ Each of the four bearers rests on the knee nearest the victim's feet. Three of the bearers position themselves on the victim's least injured side, at the victim's knees, at the hips, and at the shoulders. The fourth bearer is positioned at the victim's hips on the opposite side from the others.
- ✓ The hands of the bearer at the shoulders are placed under the victim's neck and shoulders.
- ✓ The hands of the bearer at the knees are placed under victim's knees and ankles.
- ✓ The other two bearers, across from each other, place their hands under the victim's pelvis and the small of the back.
- ✓ The four bearers slowly lift the victim, keeping the body level.
- ✓ The victim is rested on the knees of the three bearers on the same side.
- ✓ The fourth bearer then places the stretcher under the victim.
- ✓ The bearer who has placed the stretcher assumes his or her original position.
- ✓ The victim is gently lowered to the stretcher and covered with a blanket.

- ✓ The bearers position themselves, one at each end and one at each side of the stretcher, facing victim.
- ✓ All bearers grasp and lift the stretcher.
- ✓ The two bearers in the center shift one hand toward the victim's feet and support this end, while the bearer at the victim's feet turns around to a marching position.
- ✓ The victim is usually transported feet first so that the bearer at the victim's head can constantly monitor the victim's condition.

Environmental Emergencies

Hypothermia

Hypothermia is a general cooling of the entire body. The inner core of the body is chilled so the body cannot generate heat to stay warm. This condition can be produced by exposure to low temperatures or to temperatures between thirty and fifty degrees Fahrenheit with wind and rain. Also contributing to hypothermia are fatigue, hunger, and poor physical condition.

Exposure begins when the body loses heat faster than it can be produced. When the body is chilled, it passes through several stages:

- The initial response is to build a fire and voluntarily exercise in order to stay warm. The fire can also signal rescuers if the victim is lost.
- As the body tissues are cooled, the victim begins to shiver as a result of involuntary adjustment by the body to preserve normal temperature in vital organs. These responses drain the body's energy reserves.
- Cold reaches the brain and deprives the victim of judgment and reasoning powers.
- The victim experiences feelings of apathy, listlessness, indifference, and sleepiness.
- The victim does not realize what is happening.
- The victim looses muscle coordination.
- Cooling becomes more rapid as body temperature is lowered. Eventually hypothermia will result in coma. The victim will have a very slow pulse and very slow respiration. If cooling continues the victim will die.
- The victim of hypothermia may not recognize symptoms and deny that medical attention is needed; therefore, it is important to judge the symptoms rather

than what the victim says. Even mild symptoms of hypothermia need immediate medical care.

First aid for a victim of hypothermia is as follows:

- ✓ Get the victim out of the elements (wind, rain, etc.)
- ✓ Remove all wet clothing.
- ✓ Wrap the victim in blankets. Be certain the blankets are under, as well as over, the victim. Maintain the victim's body heat by building a fire or placing heat packs, electric heating pads, hot water bottles, or even another rescuer in the blankets with the victim. **(Do not warm the victim too quickly.)**
- ✓ If victim is conscious, give warm liquids to drink. If victim is conscious, try to keep the victim awake.
- ✓ CPR is indicated if the victim stops breathing and the heart stops beating.
- ✓ Get victim to a medical facility as soon as possible.
- ✓ Remember to handle the victim gently. In extreme cases rough handling may result in death.

Frostbite

Frostbite results from exposure to severe cold. It is more likely to occur when the wind is blowing, rapidly taking heat from the body. The nose, cheeks, ears, toes, and fingers are the body parts most frequently frostbitten. As a result of exposure to cold, the blood vessels constrict. Thus the blood supply to the chilled parts decreases and the tissues do not get the warmth they need.

The signs and symptoms of frostbite are not always apparent to the victim. Since frostbite has a numbing effect, the victim may not be aware of it until told by someone else.

Frostbite goes through three stages:

Frostnip

- The affected area will feel numb to the victim.
- The skin becomes red, then white during frostnip.

Treatment for frostnip is as follows:

✓ Place hand over frost nipped part.
✓ Place frost nipped fingers in armpit.

Superficial Frostbite

- As exposure continues the skin becomes white and waxy.
- Skin is firm to touch, but underlying tissues are soft.
- The exposed surface becomes numb.

The treatment for superficial frostbite is as follows:

✓ Remove the victim from the environment.
✓ Apply a steady source of external warmth.
✓ **DO NOT RUB AREA.**
✓ Cover area with a dry, sterile dressing (when dressing foot or hand, pad between toes and fingers).
✓ Splint if dealing with an extremity.
✓ Transport to the hospital.

As area thaws, it may become a mottled blue and blisters will develop.

Deep Frostbite

- If freezing is allowed to continue, all sensation is lost, and the skin becomes a "dead" white, yellow-white, or mottled blue-white.
- The skin is firm to touch as are underlying tissues.

Treatment for deep frostbite is as follows:

✓ Leave it frozen until victim reaches hospital.
✓ Dress, pad, and splint frostbitten extremities. (When dressing, pad between fingers and toes.)
✓ Transport the victim to a hospital.
✓ If there is a delay in transport, rewarming may be done at the site. Place the affected part in water bath of 100 to 105 degrees. Apply warm cloths to areas that cannot be submerged. An extreme amount of pain is associated with rewarming.
✓ Rewarming is complete when the area is warm and red or blue in color and remains so after removal

from the bath. **Do not rewarm if there is a possibility of refreezing.**

General Rules for Treating Frostbite

- ✓ Apply loose, soft, sterile dressings to affected area. Splint and elevate the extremity.
- ✓ Give the victim warm fluids containing sugar to drink if he or she does not have an altered level of consciousness.
- ✓ **Do not rub, chafe, or manipulate frostbitten parts.**
- ✓ **Do not use hot water bottles or heat lamps.**
- ✓ **Do not place victim near a stove or fire, because excessive heat can cause further tissue damage.**
- ✓ **Do not allow the victim to smoke, because nicotine constricts the blood vessels.**
- ✓ **Do not allow the victim to drink coffee, tea, or hot chocolate because these substances will cause the blood vessels to constrict.**
- ✓ **Do not allow victim to walk if feet are frostbitten.**

Heat Stroke

Heat stroke is a sudden onset of illness from exposure to the direct rays of the sun or too high temperature without exposure to the sun. Physical exertion and high humidity definitely contribute to the incidence of heat stroke.

The most important characteristic of heat stroke is the high body temperature which is caused by a disturbance in the heat-regulating mechanism of the body. The person can no longer sweat, and this causes a rise in body temperature.

This illness is more common in the elderly. Alcoholics, obese persons, and those on medication are also very susceptible to heat stroke.

The signs and symptoms of heat stroke are as follows:

- The skin is flushed, very hot, and very dry. (Perspiration is usually absent.)

- Pulse is usually strong and rapid, but may become weak and rapid as the victim's condition worsens.
- The respiration is rapid and deep, followed by shallow breathing.
- The body temperature can reach 108 degrees.
- The victim rapidly loses consciousness and may experience convulsions.

Care should be centered around lowering the body temperature as quickly as possible. Failure to do this will result in permanent brain damage or death.

The care for heat stroke is as follows:

✓ Maintain an open airway.

✓ Move the victim to a cool environment. Remove all clothing.

✓ Wrap the victim in a cool, moist sheet and use a fan to cool the victim.

✓ Immerse the victim in cool water if the above treatment is not feasible.

✓ Use cool applications if neither of above treatments are feasible.

✓ Transport the victim to the hospital as rapidly as possible, continuing cooling enroute.

Heat Exhaustion

Heat exhaustion occurs in individuals working in hot environments. It is brought about by the loss of water and salt through sweating. This loss of fluid will cause mild shock.

This illness occurs most commonly to persons not accustomed to hot weather, those who are overweight, and those who perspire excessively.

The signs and symptoms of heat exhaustion are: pale and clammy skin; skin shows evidence of profuse perspiration; breathing is rapid and shallow; pulse is rapid and weak.

The victim may complain of nausea, weakness, dizziness, and/or headache.

The first aid for heat exhaustion is as follows:

- ✓ Move the victim to a cool and comfortable place, but **do not** allow chilling.
- ✓ Try to cool the victim by fanning or wiping the face with a cool, wet cloth.
- ✓ Loosen the victim's clothing.
- ✓ If fainting seems likely, have the victim lie down with feet elevated eight to twelve inches.
- ✓ Treat the victim for shock.

Heat Cramps

Heat cramps affect people who work in a hot environment and perspire. The perspiration causes a loss of salt from the body and if there is inadequate replacement, the body will then suffer from cramps.

Signs and symptoms of heat cramps are: profuse perspiration; victim complains of muscle cramps, painful spasms in the legs or abdomen; victim may feel faint.

First aid for heat cramps is as follows:

- ✓ Move the victim to a cool environment.
- ✓ If the victim is conscious, give sips of cool salt and sugar water (one teaspoon of salt plus as much sugar as the person can stand, per quart of water) or a commercial electrolyte solution.

Medical Emergencies

Diabetic Emergencies

Body and brain cells need many different types of nourishment, one of which is sugar. The circulatory system carries sugar and transfers it to the cells with the aid of a chemical substance called insulin. The pancreas, located in the abdominal cavity, manufactures insulin. When the insulin production and sugar are in balance, the body functions normally. An individual suffering from an imbalance in the production of insulin is said to have *diabetes mellitus.*

As a result of this imbalance, the body is adversely affected. However, a great many diabetics lead healthy, normal lives through a program of balanced diet and medication. When the diabetic's condition is not controlled, certain disorders may occur. The major adverse reactions to insulin imbalance are *diabetic coma* and *insulin shock.*

Diabetic Coma

Diabetic coma is a result of an inadequate insulin supply. This imbalance is generally due to a diabetic not taking the proper medication; a diabetic ingesting more sugar than the insulin can accommodate; a person contracting an infection which affects insulin production; or a person vomiting or sustaining fluid loss.

The signs and symptoms of someone progressing into diabetic coma are:

- Warm and dry skin
- Sunken eyes
- Rapid and labored breathing
- Rapid and weak pulse
- Excessive urination
- Extreme thirst

- Nausea and vomiting
- Abdominal pain
- Sickly sweet odor of acetone (similar to nail polish remover or spoiled fruit) on the breath
- State of confusion and disorientation that is similar to drunkenness
- Eventually, a coma state, thus the term diabetic coma

First aid for the victim progressing into a diabetic coma is:

✓ Watch for vomiting.
✓ Maintain an open airway.
✓ Treat the victim for shock.
✓ Transport the victim to a medical facility as quickly as possible.

Insulin Shock

Insulin shock results when there is a shortage of sugar relative to the amount of insulin in the body. The prime reasons for the condition are that the victim has not eaten, so that not enough sugar has been taken in; the victim has taken too much insulin; or the victim has over exercised, thus burning sugar too fast.

The signs and symptoms of insulin shock are as follows:

- Victim experiences a personality change in the early stages (victims may become confused or combative)
- Headache
- Profuse perspiration
- Rapid, weak pulse
- Dizziness
- Cold, clammy skin
- Eventually, convulsions and unconsciousness
- Normal or shallow respiration

The first aid for insulin shock is as follows:

✓ If the victim is conscious, sugar can be administered in the form of orange juice, a candy bar, soft drinks, or several packets of sugar mixed with orange juice.

Don't worry about the amount of sugar given to the victim, as the doctor will balance the need for sugar against insulin production when the victim arrives at the hospital.

- ✓ If the victim is unconscious, a sprinkle of granulated sugar can be placed under the tongue.
- ✓ The victim should be transported to a medical facility for continuing care as quickly as possible.

If you cannot distinguish between a victim with insulin shock and a victim progressing into diabetic coma, give sugar to the victim. Giving sugar to a victim with too much blood sugar doesn't make any significant difference to victim outcome, but giving sugar to a victim in insulin shock can save a life.

Epileptic Seizures

Epilepsy is a neurological disorder resulting in recurring seizures. Grand mal and petit mal are the types of seizures which may occur. Of these two, grand mal is more severe.

The petit mal attack is characterized by the following:

- Only partial loss of consciousness, if any, occurs.
- Victim remains aware of what is going on nearby.
- The victim may experience minor convulsive movements of the eyes or extremities.

The signs and symptoms of a grand mal seizure are:

- The victim may have a premonition or aura before the attack occurs.
- Loss of consciousness occurs.
- The victim's body becomes rigid, and then convulsions occur.
- During the seizure, the victim may lose bowel and bladder control.
- The face is usually pale before the seizure and becomes cyanotic (bluish) during the seizure.
- Severe spasms of the jaw muscles sometimes occur,

causing the tongue to be bitten.

- Breathing may be loud and labored with a peculiar hissing sound or it may stop during the seizure.
- The victim may froth at the mouth.

The seizure only lasts for a few minutes. The victim usually will be unconscious for a period of time after the seizure. After the seizure the victim will usually be very tired and sleepy.

If the victim does not regain consciousness after the seizure and begins to experience more convulsions, the patient is in a more critical situation.

The following first aid for a victim of an epileptic seizure should be given as necessary:

✓ The victim should be kept calm. **Do not** restrain the victim.

✓ Protect the victim from injury by moving objects that could cause harm.

✓ **Do not** place anything in the victim's mouth during the seizure.

When the seizure is over, do the following:

✓ Maintain an open airway.

✓ Allow the victim to rest.

✓ Protect the victim from stress or embarrassment.

Stroke

A stroke occurs when the blood supply carrying oxygen to the brain is cut off due to a blockage or rupture of a blood vessel. The effects of a stroke on the brain can be temporary or permanent, and range from slight to severe.

Cerebral thrombosis is a blockage of the cerebral artery by a clot which forms inside the artery.

Cerebral hemorrhage occurs when a diseased artery in the brain ruptures and floods the surrounding tissue with blood.

Cerebral embolism occurs when a wandering blood

clot (embolus) carried in the blood stream becomes lodged in one of the cerebral blood vessels.

The signs and symptoms of a stroke are as follows:

- The victim may have a decreased level of consciousness or be totally unconscious.
- Respiration is usually slow with a snoring sound caused by the tongue falling back into the airway.
- Pupils are unequal in size.
- Paralysis or weakness on one side of the body or face is present.
- The victim loses the ability to speak, or the victim's speech is slurred.

The first aid for a stroke victim is as follows:

✓ Maintain an open airway.

✓ Keep the tongue or saliva from blocking the air passage.

✓ **Do not** give the victim anything by mouth.

✓ Keep the victim lying down with the head and shoulders raised to alleviate some of the pressure on the brain. If the victim is unconscious, place the victim on the affected side to allow fluids to drain.

✓ **Do not** move the victim any more than necessary.

✓ Keep the victim quiet and calm.

✓ Reassure the victim, who may be quite anxious or nervous.

✓ Obtain medical care as soon as possible.

DRUG ABUSE

Drugs may be classified as uppers, downers, narcotics, mind-affecting (hallucinogens), or volatile chemicals.

Uppers are stimulants that affect the nervous system to excite the user.

Downers are depressants that affect the central nervous system and relax the user.

Narcotics affect the nervous system and change many

of the normal activities of the body and often produces an intense state of excitement or distortion of the user's senses.

Volatile chemicals are depressants acting upon the central nervous system.

It is important for the first aider to be able to detect possible drug abuse at the overdose level and to relate certain signs to certain types of drugs. You will use basically the same care for all drug abuse victims and that care will not change unless you are ordered to do something by a poison control center.

Signs of Drug Abuse

Drug abuse and drug overdose signs and symptoms can vary from one victim to another, even for the same drug. The scene, bystanders, and the victim may be your only sources for finding out if you are dealing with drug abuse and the substance involved. When questioning the victim and bystanders, ask if the victim has been taking any medications rather than using the word *drugs*.

The following significant signs and symptoms are related to specific drugs:

Uppers: Excitement, increased pulse and breathing rates, rapid speech, dry mouth, dilated pupils, sweating, and the complaint of having gone without sleep for long periods.

Downers: Sluggish, sleepy victim lacking typical coordination of body movements and speaking with slurred speech. Pulse and breathing rates are low, often to the point of a true emergency.

Mind-affecting drugs; Fast pulse rate, dilated pupils, and a flushed face. The victim often "sees" things, has little concept of real time, and may not be aware of the true environment. Often, the victim makes no sense when speaking.

Narcotics: Reduced rate of pulse and breathing, often has a lower skin temperature. The pupils are constricted, muscles are relaxed, and sweating is heavy. The victim is very sleepy and may go into a coma.

Volatile chemicals: Dazed or showing temporary loss of contact with reality. The victim may go into a coma. The inside of the nose and mouth may show swollen membranes. The victim may complain of a "funny numb feeling" or "tingling" inside the head.

Some of the above symptoms are similar to other medical emergencies previously discussed.

Care for Drug Abuse Victims

When providing care for drug abuse victims, you should:

- ✓ Summon help so that an ambulance or a physician may be called to the scene.
- ✓ Monitor breathing and be alert for respiratory arrest.
- ✓ Talk to the victim to gain confidence and to maintain the level of consciousness.
- ✓ Protect the victim from further harm.
- ✓ Treat for shock.
- ✓ Continue to reassure the victim throughout all phases of care.

NOTE: You should always be alert and ready to protect yourself since many drug abusers appear calm at first and then become violent as time passes. If the victim creates an unsafe scene and you are not a trained law enforcement officer, GET OUT and find a safe place until the police arrive.

POISONS

Poisons are any substances which act to produce harmful effects on the normal body processes. There are four ways in which these substances may enter the body:

- Ingestion
- Inhalation
- Injection
- Absorption

Poisoning by Ingestion

The chief causes of poisoning by ingestion are as follows:

- Overdose of medication (intentional or accidental). This includes the combining of drugs and alcohol.
- Household cleaners, chemicals and medications left within the reach of children
- Original labels left on containers that are now used to store poisons
- Improperly stored food

The signs and symptoms of poisoning by ingestion are:

- Nausea, vomiting, and diarrhea
- Severe abdominal pains or cramps
- Altered respiration and pulse rates
- Corroded, burned, or destroyed tissues of the mouth
- Unusual odors on the breath
- Stains around the mouth

The following is first aid for poisoning by ingestion:

✓ Call the poison control center.

✓ The control center may indicate to dilute the substance by giving the victim milk or water or induce vomiting so that the substance is removed from the stomach.

✓ Vomiting should **NOT** be induced in the following cases:

✓ If the victim has swallowed a strong acid or alkali

which would cause further damage when vomited.

- ✓ If a petroleum product has been swallowed, because it can be easily inhaled into the lungs and cause pneumonia
- ✓ If the victim is unconscious or semiconscious because victim may inhale the vomit into the lungs
- ✓ If the victim is convulsing
- ✓ If the victim has a serious heart problem

Check with the poison control center to determine the best method to induce vomiting. The victim should be sitting and leaning forward to prevent vomit from going into the lungs. Collect the vomit and take it to the hospital with the victim, along with the poison's container.

Poisoning by Inhalation

Certain toxic or noxious gases may stop respiration by a direct poisoning effect or by preventing the transport of oxygen by the red blood cells. Such gases are encountered in mining, oil drilling, and similar industries. They include sulfur dioxide, the oxides of nitrogen, ammonia, hydrogen sulfide, hydrogen cyanide, and carbon monoxide.

The signs and symptoms of inhaled poisons are:

- Shortness of breath
- Coughing
- Cyanosis (bluish color)
- Cherry red color if dealing with carbon monoxide poisoning

To provide first aid, proceed as follows:

- ✓ Remove victim to fresh air as quickly as possible. The rescuer should not risk entering a hazardous atmosphere without proper protective equipment.
- ✓ Maintain an open airway.
- ✓ In appropriate cases, initiate artificial ventilation or cardiopulmonary resuscitation.
- ✓ Treat the victim for shock.

Carbon Monoxide Carbon monoxide, a product of incomplete combustion is probably the most common of the poisonous gases. Overexposure can be fatal. Carbon monoxide causes asphyxia because it combines with the hemoglobin of the blood much more readily than oxygen does. The blood, therefore, carries less and less oxygen from the lungs to the body tissues. The first symptoms of asphyxia appear when a thirty percent blood saturation level has been reached.

The signs and symptoms of carbon monoxide poisoning are:

- Headache
- Dizziness
- Yawning
- Fainting
- Weakness
- Bright, cherry red color
- Lips and earlobes may possibly turn bluish in color
- Nausea and vomiting

To provide first aid for carbon monoxide poisoning proceed as for any other inhalation poisoning.

Poisoning by Absorption

Many substances in the form of gases, fumes, mists, liquids, and dusts cause poisoning or irritation of the skin when they come into contact with it. Underlying tissues (hair follicles, oil glands, sweat glands) may also be affected. The normal structure of the skin is changed and irritation and inflammation occur. Usually, inflammation does not progress rapidly, but gradually, after continued exposure to the cause. Persons who note changes in the normal texture of their skin or continued irritation of the skin should seek medical advice before a chronic condition develops. Needless discomfort can be prevented by early medical care.

First aid for the victim of contact poisoning is as follows:

- ✓ Remove contaminated clothing.
- ✓ Flood the contaminated area with plenty of water.
- ✓ If dealing with a dry poison, brush as much off as possible before washing the area with water.
- ✓ Watch the person for signs of shock and changes in respiration.

Poisoning by Injection

Poisons can enter the skin by means of injections or bites of animals, poisonous snakes, and insects. Some people may have an allergic reaction to a nonpoisonous insect bite or drug which may result in anaphylactic shock.

First aid is aimed at minimizing the travel of the poison to the heart. General first aid for poisons injected into the skin is as follows:

- ✓ Keep the person calm, quiet, and at rest.
- ✓ All jewelry (bracelets, rings, watches, etc.) should be removed from the extremity, in case of swelling.
- ✓ Apply a constricting bandage above and below the bite at the edge of the swelling, loosely enough to slide a finger under the bandage. Pulse should be checked periodically below the bite; bandages are used only as a constriction, not as a tourniquet.
- ✓ Transport the victim to a medical facility while keeping the victim as calm and as still as possible.

Bites of Animals

Any warm-blooded animal may suffer from rabies. If a person is bitten by an animal, always suspect the animal to be rabid until it is proven otherwise. The saliva from a rabid animal enters the wound caused by the bite, transmitting the disease to the victim. If possible the animal should be captured or identified and held for medical observation.

First aid for animal bites is as follows:

- ✓ Control bleeding.

✓ Wash the wound with soap and water and rinse with alcohol.
✓ Dress and bandage the wound. Splint if dealing with an extremity.
✓ Take the victim to a medical facility as quickly as possible.

Snakebites

Coral snakes, copperheads, rattlesnakes, and water moccasins are the four types of poisonous snakes in the United States.

The signs and symptoms of a snakebite are:

- Sharp, stinging pain with one or more puncture marks in the area
- Swelling
- Discoloration
- Pain in the bitten area

As the poison goes through the body, other symptoms develop such as:

- Weakness
- Nausea and vomiting
- Weak and rapid pulse
- Respiratory distress
- Shock

The first aid for snakebites is as follows:

✓ Begin care at once.
✓ Keep victim lying down and quiet with the injured part immobile and lower than the rest of the body.
✓ Remove all rings, watches, etc. from the extremity.
✓ Apply constricting bands above and below the area. The constricting bands should be tight enough to slow down surface circulation but not so tight as to cut off arterial flow.
✓ Treat for shock.
✓ Apply an ice pack to the wound **only** if the poison

control center or a physician advises to do so. **Do not** cut into the bite and suction or squeeze unless you are directed to do so by a physician. **NEVER** suck the venom from the wound using your mouth.

- ✓ **Do not** give the victim anything by mouth.
- ✓ Identify the snake if possible. If the snake can be killed, take it to the hospital with the victim.
- ✓ Monitor vital signs while transporting victim to a medical facility.

For persons who frequent regions infested with poisonous snakes, it is recommended that a snakebite kit be carried.

Insect Bites and Stings

Many insects bite or sting, but few can cause serious symptoms by themselves, unless of course, the person is allergic to them. However, some insects transmit diseases. For example, certain types of mosquitoes transmit malaria, yellow fever, and other diseases; certain types of ticks transmit spotted or Rocky Mountain fever; and certain types of biting flies transmit tularemia or rabbit fever.

Occasionally, stinging or biting insects that have been feeding on or have been in contact with poisonous substances can transmit this poison at the time of the sting or bite.

Persons who have experienced serious reactions from previous insect bites should be urged to secure any possible immunization or have an antidote readily available to prevent more serious reactions from future bites and stings.

The signs and symptoms of insect bites and stings are:

- The stings of bees and the bites of mosquitoes, ticks, fleas, and bedbugs usually cause only local irritation and pain in the region stung or bitten.
- Moderate swelling and redness may occur and some itching, burning, and pain may be present.

The first aid for insect bites and stings is as follows:

- ✓ The sting area should be inspected to determine whether the stinger is still left in the body. If it is, remove it in order to prevent further injection of toxin. The stinger should be carefully scraped off the skin, rather than grasped with tweezers, so as not to squeeze toxin into the body.
- ✓ Application of ice or ice water to the bite helps to slow absorption of toxin into the blood stream. A paste of baking soda and water can also be applied.
- ✓ The victim should be observed for signs of an allergic reaction. For people who are allergic, maintain an open airway and get the victim to medical help as quickly as possible.

Bites and Stings of Spiders, Centipedes, Tarantulas, and Scorpions

The effect of stings and bites of spiders, centipedes, tarantulas, and scorpions in some instances are much more severe than those of the insects previously mentioned. They may cause alarming symptoms.

The signs and symptoms of these bites are as follows:

- Generally, the bite consists of two small pinpoint punctures of the skin and produce local swelling and redness with a smarting, burning pain.
- Exhaustion, sweating, and nausea may appear.
- Pain or cramping may develop in the back, shoulders, chest, and limbs.
- In some instances the symptoms are mild and subside within six to twelve hours, but occasionally they are severe and can cause a state of collapse.

The **black widow spider** is a moderately large, glossy black spider with very fine hairs over the body, which give it a silky appearance. On the abdomen is a characteristic red or crimson marking in the form of an hourglass. Only the female is poisonous; the smaller male is harmless.

The **brown recluse spider** injects a venom which causes a limited destruction of red blood cells and certain other blood changes. The victim may develop chills, fever, joint pains, nausea, and vomiting. A rash may also develop within twenty-four to forty-eight hours.

Tarantulas are hairy spiders. Those found in the southwestern United States are not poisonous, but occasionally a victim will have an allergic reaction to the injected venom. Tarantulas coming into the country in imported fruit may be poisonous. Their bites may cause marked pain and local redness with swelling. Death is extremely rare.

Most species of **scorpions** in this country do not inject a toxin that is generally harmful to humans. The sting may result in local swelling and discoloration, similar to a wasp sting, and may sometimes cause allergic reactions. The sting of the more dangerous species of scorpions causes little or no swelling or discoloration, but locally there will be a tingling or burning sensation. Considerable discomfort may ensue. Death, although unlikely, occurs occasionally in infants and young children and might conceivably occur in older persons. The poison acts mainly on the nervous system.

The first aid for an allergic reaction to bites and stings of spiders, centipedes, tarantulas and scorpions is as follows:

- ✓ Apply constricting band between the bite or sting and the heart if the bite is on an extremity.
- ✓ Apply a cold pack on the area.
- ✓ Keep the victim quiet to retard absorption of the poison into the circulatory system.
- ✓ If the bite is on an extremity, splint it and keep it lower than the heart.
- ✓ Get victim to medical help as quickly as possible.

Poison Ivy, Poison Oak, and Poison Sumac

These poisonous plants grow as vines or shrubs, from ankle to shoulder high. The poison comes mainly from their leaves but also may come from bruising their roots, stems, and berries. The smoke from burning brush containing these plants has been known to carry the poisons a considerable distance.

The signs and symptoms of this kind of skin poisoning are:

- A red rash, with some swelling, itching and burning, followed by formation of blisters of various sizes filled with blood serum.
- The symptoms appear on the exposed skin surfaces, usually the hands, wrists and arms, six hours to several days after exposure.
- The blisters may fill with pus or contaminated fluid. When they break, crusts and scabs are formed. Considerable fluid may exude from broken blisters.
- When the affected area is large and the inflammation is severe, there may be fever, headache, and general body weakness.

The first aid for the victim of such poisoning is as follows:

✓ Contaminated clothing and jewelry should be removed.

✓ Wash the area with soap and water.

✓ A lotion may be applied to ease the victim's discomfort, if the rash is mild.

✓ If a severe reaction appears, seek medical help.